Black and Colored Women of the Bible

By:

Bishop Charles K. Aka
&
Theresa A. Liptrot

ISBN: 1-4033-9503-9 (E-book)
ISBN: 1-4033-9504-7 (Paperback)

This book is printed on acid free paper.

1stBooks – rev. 04/08/03

DEDICATION

This book is in memory of my beloved Aunt, Princess Elizabeth Baidoo (a.k.a.) Adwoa Anokono for her profound love, devotion and good foundation she laid, which have tremendously affected both my advancement and success and the working out of God's will in my life. May the Lord God bless and keep her till we meet in His glorious kingdom.

With all my love,
Bishop Charles K. Aka

The daughter of Rose Lee (Norris) Artemus dedicates this co-authored book to her. Mommy this is for your courage, devotion, sacrifices, and most of all, love. During times that were bitterly difficult, you always gave all of yourself to your eight children, and never faltered. Your inner strength and spirit is admired and I pray that God has blessed me with the gifts He gave you, which held life altogether for all of us. Thank you, may God continue to bless you in these ripe years.

With all my love,
Theresa Artemus-
Liptrot

TABLE OF CONTENTS

PREFACE

The total injustices and dishonor done to black, colored or gentile women of the Bible by preachers, and teachers, both men and women alike, is a disservice and an unfortunate unbiblical mistake that needs to be corrected. It is for this purpose, that this powerful new book "Black and Colored Women of the Bible" has been written. I know for sure that the critics (even many of my brethren in the Lord) may not appreciate and welcome my opinion about the topic. I faithfully have written this book because I have been led by the Lord to do so.

By the power of His Spirit, I have been chosen as a vessel, to rebuild the lives of these noble women of the Holy Bible, and to learn and spiritually grow from it. I fervently pray that He will mercifully fill any shortcomings, if any.

I strongly hope that at least some precious, seeking souls will read what is presented and be directed toward the Lord Jesus Christ whom is the only source of truth and salvation.

My prayer again is that, "the Lord will give the reader understanding in all things" and "use these humble endeavors for his Glory" (2 Timothy 2:7; Peter 4:11)

ACKNOWLEDGEMENTS

First, I very much thank my Lord who has led me along diverse ways, always protecting, loving, strengthening and overpoweringly drawing me close to him. He is my strength, wisdom, song, and my teacher. To my best and beloved friends Brenda Francis, Theresa Artemus and her precious husband Kenneth Liptrot, without their assistance, faith, patience and encouragement my books would not have risen from a dream to a reality. My special thanks goes to Minister CeAnn McFarland, Dina Garbarah Sam, and Sherlan A. Thomas, MSN, FNP, of Montefiore Medical Center, for their profound love, care and direction. I am indebted to all my friends both at home and abroad who have encouraged me in many ways. Last, but not least, I am thankful to my precious children and my entire family for their love, encouragement, support, and patience to accomplish this wealthy course.

Bishop Charles K. Aka

I praise God for bringing me through yet another part of a journey that I did not know I was on until it was over. He provided people in the path of His glory to help me. I know they love me and would do anything for me but I must be sure that they know from my heart; I send out a grand thank you to my husband Kenneth and my mother Rose, they supported me through the hard times when I needed it the most. As I work my way towards the end of this particular journey, I would also like to thank my friend Sandra Da'Silva. Your support was needed and appreciated and I thank God for sending you my way on those special days, thank you for your obedient servitude to the Lord.

Theresa A. Liptrot

Chapter One

Introduction

"But there went up a mist from earth, and watered the whole face of the ground. And the Lord God formed man of the dust of the ground, and breathed into his nostrils the breath of life; and man became a living soul." (Genesis 2:6-7)

The scriptures as stated above explain that, streams (vapor) went up from the ground and watered the earth. The Lord God took a handful of soil and made a man. He later breathed life into the man he had made. He perfectly created man, and man became a living being.

We all do agree that, the color of our planet earth's soil from the beginning of its creation is dark brown or black (in a vague term). Scientists have discovered that other planets have different colors and types of soil, but it has never been reported

1

that they have found the color of "white". Therefore, from the holy and historical record of Genesis, we could boldly and honestly say that, the color of our first parents Adam and Eve was either dark brown or black, and not light or white in color. A conscious review of scriptures will lead to clearer understanding that, even the Savior Jesus Christ who was referred to as Emmanuel (meaning God with us) was dark or black in complexion. The book of Daniel, Ezekiel, and Revelation describe the Son of God (Jesus) as God incarnate, with hair like "wool," and with bodily parts the color of "brass" and "amber." (Daniel 7:9; Ezekiel 1:27; 8:2; Revelation 1:14-15)

To support my argument, we all do accept that, since the beginning of this awesome world, it is always the black or colored couples who gave birth to "albinos," (I mean people with pure white skin and hair), but we have never seen white couples giving birth to a child with pure black skin and hair.

Hence, I sincerely and boldly say, "yes!" black is the original color of mankind. All white and colored people originated from black people. Therefore, blacks are the progenitors of humanity and the creative originators of culture and civilization.

"The Lord caused a deep sleep to fall upon Adam, and he slept: and he took one of his ribs, and closed up the flesh instead thereof; And the rib which the Lord God had taken from man, made he a woman, and brought her unto the man. And Adam said, this is now bone of my bones, and flesh of my flesh: she shall be called Woman, because she was taken out of Man. Therefore shall a man leave his father and his mother, and shall cleave unto his wife: and they shall be one flesh." (Genesis 2:21-24)

Since the creation of our beautiful planet, our Lord God has seriously involved women of all races and generations in His divine and perfect plan for man. Eve was presented to Adam for a purpose. The infinite mind of the Almighty God made woman as both helper and a companion for man. It is truly impossible to separate woman from man because woman came out of man. (Genesis 2:23) This is one of the reasons that Adam yielded to his wife Eve (his own bone and flesh) and sinned against God and they both fell. It is directly true that if one part of the body is weak, the whole body is affected. The same thing happens if one part of the body is strong, the whole body is affected. (1Corinthians 12:26) Eve as a part of Adam's body was weak.

So far as biblical men and women marriage relationships are concerned, one quality has remained with black and colored (African) women: They are sincerely spiritual women. There are many spirited black and colored women in the Holy Scriptures likewise in history. However, we shall talk about only a few of them in this book. The Gospel of John (John 20:30-31) validates the above statement. Here are a few of the unique Black and Colored women found in the Holy Scriptures: Eve, Hagar, Keturah, Tamar, Asenath, Zipporah, Rahab, Delilah, Ruth, and the historical Bathsheba of Uriah, and even the spiritless Delilah were used to further God's plan. Many of them were women of courage, hope, hardwork, faith, love, respect, sympathy, humility, honesty, generosity, beauty and above all showed faith in action along with their intuitive womanly spirit.

A significant feature of this book shows that these women were used for the purposes of God's spiritual goodness, God's will, and perfect glory that paved the way for the fruition of our black descendants.

The characteristics of these black and colored women will begin to unfold when we reveal later about each one of their moral, physical, psychological, spiritual, and religious points of view. We will relate God's will that allowed the involvement of these women in the lives of some of the great and God-chosen men in the Holy Scriptures, whom fulfilled His divine and perfect plan for man. I humbly pray that upon reading the following scriptures that you will begin to see the merciful and loving God's plan for all of us that believe and call on Christ as their Savior.

"Then Peter opened his mouth, and said, of a truth I perceive that God is no respecter of person: But in every nation he that feareth Him, and worketh righteousness, is accepted with Him." (Acts 10:34-35; Romans 2:11; Samuel 16:7.)

First, the word of God vividly explains that, our good God does not have any favorites. The Lord is only pleased with everyone that believes and worships him and does right, no matter what color, language, and nation one comes from.

Secondly, we should bear in mind that God allowed these black and colored women to become involved in the lives of His chosen servants because He found them to be useful in fulfilling his glorious prophecy to free humankind from the bondage of sin and the illusions that the world captured them under through truth and righteousness. In short, these women had spiritual qualities and were intended to marry the men of God to become mothers to men sought to open the way to the coming of God's only begotten son. In the book of proverbs, King Solomon explained the character of a God-fearing woman and wife.

"A truly good woman and wife is the precious treasure a man can find. She is dependable and very good always to her husband. She helps with the furnishing of clothing, money and food to the house. She gets up early in the morning to prepare food for her family and strangers. She is hardworking and helps both the poor and the needy. She is neat, cheerful and respectful. Her words are sensible and her advice thoughtful. She takes good care of her family, never lazy and shows optimistic hope for the future. Her children praise her, and with great pride her husband says, "There are many good women but you are the best." Lastly, she fears the Lord."

"Charm can be deceiving and beauty fades away, but a woman who honors the Lord deserves to be praised." (Proverbs 31:10-30 CEV). The great Apostle Paul also said, Women were created to bring glory and honor to men. (1 Corinthians 11:17)

In examining the above stated scriptures we clearly see the same qualities in the lives of the religious black and colored women in the Holy Book. God is truly omnipotent; God knows why these particular women became part and parcel, blessed as vessels of wife, mother, grandmother, and great grandmother's of godly men in biblical times, for His own glory.

The Word of God says, "The secret things belong unto the Lord our God. But those things which are revealed belong unto us and to our children for ever, that we may do all the words of the law". (Deuteronomy 29:29)

In this context, we are told that, the Lord our God sometimes does not explain the present or the future. He sometimes does not show how and why He does things, but all we have to do is accept whole-heartedly and humbly obey His commandments with our children and be abundantly blessed. It is our good God who knows what is the best for us all. "The Lord's thoughts and His ways are not like ours" (Isaiah 55:8)

Everything the Lord does is for our betterment and eternal salvation. We can strongly voice that if it was first through the fault of a woman (EVE) that our first parents sinned against the Almighty God and all mankind fell, then, it is definitely right but not wrong for God to also involve women of all races in His perfect plan of salvation for all men. (Ephesians 2:11-22)

Now, if people still think that God only involved white and black Hebrew or Jewish women like Sarah, Rebecca, Leah, Rachel, Hannah, Naomi, Esther, Huldah, Deborah, Miriam, and many others in the lives of his chosen servants without involving also the black and colored women from the "gentile" world, then, that could only mean that our Lord God has been grossly partial in His perfect plan of salvation for all humankind.

Undoubtedly, the involvement of black and colored women in the lives of godly men in the biblical times had tremendously assisted the biblical truth and the completion of the genealogy of the Lord and Savior Jesus Christ whom is the chief corner-stone of our victory and salvation. (1Peter 2:6) It is evident in the first chapter of the book of Mathew that, the four important gentile (black and colored) women by name Rahab, Tamar, Ruth, and Bathsheba were the great ancestors of our Lord Jesus Christ.

We faithfully understand and conclude that the workings of God are all good and His will is perfect, God is good and perfect for our spiritual growth and eternal salvation in Christ Jesus.

BRIEF BACKGROND OF BLACK & COLORED PEOPLE

"He ... hath made of one blood all nations of men for to dwell on all the face of the earth, and hath determined the times before appointed, and the bounds of their habitation." (Acts 17:26)

It is the will of God to decide when and where every nation on earth should be. Then all Black (African) including the colored people both in the motherland and in the diaspora should be grateful, joyful and satisfied with where the Creator of all things placed them. He our Lord God only knows the best for the rich and the poor, for the young and old, and for people of all colors and non-colors.

"The earth and everything on it belong to the Lord. The world and its people belong to Him. And the Lord placed it all in the oceans and rivers. (Psalm 24:1-2).

From the holy scriptures and historical record of Genesis 5:32, 9:18, 10:1, 6, 10 and 32, we learn that, Ham who was the second son, his two brothers Shem and Japheth, their three wives, including their beloved and very religious father Noah and mother, only remained on this earth following or after the great flood. From these eight people the whole world was repopulated.

Concerning Ham, he became the father of four children called Mizram (Egypt), Put (Libya), Cush (Ethiopia), and Canaan (Palestine). Ham also called Kemit, became the ancestor of all "Black" or "Hamitic" people on earth. He was himself black and his four sons founded their own nations and also gave birth to other black peoples. Now, let us restrict ourselves to the descendants of Ham and their nations or kingdoms on the earth.

Mizram means red soil. He was the second son of Ham and founded one of the ancient's great and civilized nations named Egypt also known as Coptic land. He became the ancestor of Ludim, Anamim, Lehabim, Naphtuhim, Pathrusim, Casluhim, and his grandson Caphturim was also the ancestor of the

Philistines. According to the Bible, the offspring of Ham, the great ancestor of all blacks or Hamitic races first populated Egypt.

Canaan means low. He was fourth son of Ham. He founded the land of Canaan also named Palestine, which later became the "Holy Land" for the Israelites. Canaan was the ancestor of the Jebusites, the Amorites, the Girgashites, the Hivites, the Arkites, the Sinites, the Arvadites, the Zemarites, and the Hamathites. His children were Sidon the first born, and Heth the second born. Heth was very great and famous and became the father of the Hittites. All these people were black and became part of the "gentile" world in biblical times. Later the Canaanites spread from the territory of Sidon and went far as Gaza in the direction of Gerar. They also went as far as Lasha in the direction of Sodom, Gomorrah, Admah, and Zeboim.

Cush means black. He was the first son of Ham and founded the oldest empire of Ethiopia. Cush also called Kush was the ancestor of the Cushites. Cush's sons were Seba, Havilah, Sabtah, Raamah, and Sebteca. His son Raamah gave birth to the two famous sons called Sheba and Dedan. Cush was also the father of the great and powerful Nimrod. Nimrod, according to scriptures was an ancient Emperor, a mighty hunter, warrior and builder, whose strength or power came from the Lord God. He founded and also effectively ruled Babylon and Assyria. Nimrod built the magnificent cities like Rehoboth-Ir, Resen, Calah, Erech, Accad, Calneh and Babel, where the ancient awesome "Tower" was built. These cities were all in the Land of Shinar (probably inclusive of Babylon and Mesopotamia, the alluvian plain through which the Tigris and Euphrates rivers pass.) He also built the great and the Biblical City of Nineveh in Assyria. Nimrod also founded the old Sumerian civilization in Southern Asia of Cushite origin, and had cultural connections or relationship with Egyptian civilization. The Sumerians were composed of people who were the indigenous population of Mesopotamia and called themselves "The Blackheads." Their origin was Cushite (Ethiopian).

From the record of the scriptures, we can boldly claim that Babylon, Assyria, Egypt, Ethiopia, Canaan (the entire coast of Palestine and Phoenicia) and for that matter Libya were originally populated by the Blacks (Africans). This statement is true because both the Holy Scripture and history of the world have diametrically confirmed that claim.

Phut means bow. He was the third son of Ham. Phut also named Put founded the nation of Libya and was very great and powerful man in history. Phut was the father of the Lubim or Lehabim tribe.

Today, if surprisingly we see "white" races dominate these ancient nations once inhabited by pure "black" people, it was because of the successive foreign invasions and conquests and also the unwanted crossbreeding between whites and once enslaved blacks. Again, the total extermination of the black population by the notorious conquerors from their ancient inhabited lands had contributed immensely to this unfortunate situation. This continuous crossbreeding has also brought many colored people on earth.

Upon the true account of the Holy Scriptures and the world history, people still doubt or argue strongly that, Christ Jesus who is the Savior of all men was a pure "white" Israelite. If He was, then Jesus Christ might well have inherited genes from black ancestors, which would have made Him a black person. We thank God so much for His plan of assimilation and salvation.

We are happy that, the victory of the monogenetic theory of humanity compels one to accept that all races descended from the Black race, consistent with a filiation process that science will one day expound upon.

Finally, we sincerely iterate that, there is not an atom of lie in either history or biblical records that assert that, Egyptians, Libyans, Ethiopians, and Canaanites were of the same race.

Chapter Two

The Story of EVE

After God perfectly made all of His creation including Adam who was put in the Garden of Eden, He rested from his work the seventh day. God later found that, it was not good for the blessed Adam to live alone, because all the living creatures He created had their partners. The woman made for Adam was named Eve.

"The Lord God said, "It is not good for the man to live alone. I need to make a suitable partner for him"-----So the Lord God made man (Adam) fall into a deep sleep, and He took out one of the man's ribs. Then after closing the man's side, the Lord made a woman out of the rib: The Lord God brought her to the man, and the man exclaimed, "Here is someone like me! She is part of my body, my own flesh and bones. She came from me, a man. I will name her a Woman!" (Genesis 2:18, 21-23 CEV)

15

To portray Eve's story is to tell the history of our existence, and that is at the beginning, our creation. Eve means life. She was the mother of all living. She was the first woman made out of man and became Adam's partner in the Garden of Eden. God gave both Adam and Eve custody of the earth and of all things. Eve was perfect and the most beautiful woman that ever existed. There is not much of a story to reference about Eve, the woman. However, what we are able to say with confidence is that once the sin of Adam and Eve had been committed, it resulted in a punishment from God that resulted in both Adam and Eve being cast out of the 'Garden of Eden'.

So as we begin, we unfold the beginning. If the first parent (Adam) as told by the Holy Scriptures was created out of the dark brown or black dust, then, our great grandmother Eve was a dark or black woman, and we should not feel the need to argue over this fact. Eve was God's best, and last gift, the crowning act of His whole amazing creation. Not like Abraham the Hebrew, Jacob the father of the Israelites, and Ishmael the progenitor of Ishmaelites or Arabian tribes; Eve and Adam lived on this beautiful planet without a tribe or race. Eve was the most affectionate and blessed mother on earth. As woman, Eve was given all the tools needed to be a helpmate to Adam. She was created from the rib that was attached to Adam's spine. The creator was giving Adam another backbone of which he could rely upon. Eve as woman, also possessed inner qualities that allowed her to be emotionally supporting, loving, and nurturing. Her creation takes on the same wonder as that of all other things, which God created and called good.

Eve was formed in all human perfection, even perfect in intelligence, shining loveliness and celestial beauty, because she came from the hands of the Creator. She was the first woman to have marriage on our awesome planet with Adam, which was performed by the Almighty God. They became the first couple; she was the first bride, wife, mother (of every living soul) and grandmother. Like Adam, Eve was a partaker of the "Divine Image" of the Lord God and had dominion over all the works of God's hands. She was the only queen of the Universe. Eve was both the glory and the crown of Adam.

"For a man indeed ought not to cover his head, since he is the image and glory of God; but woman is the glory of man. For man is not from woman, but woman from man. Nor was man created for woman, but woman for the man." (1Corinthians 11:7-9).

"An excellent wife is the crown of her husband, but she who causes shame is like rottenness in his bone." (Proverbs 12:4).

It is obviously true that, man is the head of a woman. Nevertheless, the woman is always a crown and glory to her husband. The great and the real truth is not only that Eve came from the rib of Adam, but that God Almighty created her and brought the reality of her womanhood into being.

The magnificent subject of the story is that, God seeing the incompleteness of man standing alone in the Garden of Eden, He thought it wise and perfect to create a helpmate for him. God was compelled to make for man a helpmate who was his equal and shared in the process of creation. Hence, God created this helpmate Eve from the rib of Adam. The representation of the rib is that, it was taken from the place nearest to Adam's heart, thus indicating the close relationship of man and woman. Man and woman were created for each other, woman, bone of man's bone and flesh of man's flesh. For this reason, both Adam and Eve were not all that complete until they were together. In a true marriage, the oneness of man and woman come into its fullest meaning.

"Therefore, shall a man leave his father and his mother, and shall cleave unto his wife: and they shall be one flesh." (Genesis 2:24)

This confirms the reasoning that man needs to leave his father's family or home, of which he is born, and bond with his rib, which is his woman and builds his own home and tends to his own family in that home. Marriage exists not as a civil contract, which many may think about, but as a divine institution. In this union of Adam and Eve, all marriages become equal or the same with creation. It proves that the laws of morals and the laws of nature are bound together and therefore are the same.

The true happiness in marriage is not found on material things. The requirements for happiness in marriage is that each find God's gift in the other partner and unconditional love for each other. This is because loving is giving, unchanging giving of oneself for and to the other. That is, thinking about one another at all times.

In the account of Genesis, Eve is raised to celestial beauty and noble dignity, a symbol of her true worth. In Adam's family, the joy and unhappiness came into being with Eve at the center of it. In Eve also, all the fundamental questions of life, birth, temptation, sin, and even death, stands out or presents itself in its human measurement.

"Now the serpent was more subtle than any beast of the field which the Lord God had made. And he said unto the woman, Yea, hath God said, ye shall not eat of every tree of the garden? And the woman said unto the serpent, we may eat of the fruit of the trees of the garden: But of the fruit of the tree which is in the midst of the garden, God hath said, Ye shall not eat of it, neither shall ye touch it, least ye die. And the serpent said unto the woman, ye shall not surely die: For God doth know that in the day ye eat thereof, then your eyes shall opened, and ye shall be gods, knowing good and evil. And when the woman saw that the tree was good for food, and that it was pleasant to the eyes, and a tree to be desired to make one wise, she took of the fruit thereof, and did eat and gave also unto her husband with her; and he did eat. And the eyes of them both were opened; and they knew that they were naked; and they sewed fig leaves together, and made themselves aprons. And they heard the voice of the Lord God walking in the garden in the cool of the day: and Adam and his wife hid themselves from the presence of the Lord God amongst the trees of the garden." (Genesis 3:1-8)

The devil knew already that, the Lord God created man as morally responsible being with a free will to serve Him. The tempter intentionally entered one day the garden to test Adam and Eve. When Eve listened to the serpent, symbolizing trial, she followed not the will of God but the direction of evil. When she ate the fruit from the "Forbidden Tree", she disobeyed God in whose image she had been created. Instead of obeying the Creator of all things who had her interest at heart, she turned to a serpent that distorted the truth in respect of the fruit God had forbidden. The serpent deceived Eve by telling her that if she would eat of the forbidden fruit, she would be enlightened as God Himself. After Eve had eaten of the forbidden fruit, she gave it to her beloved husband and partner Adam, and he too ate it. Thus, Adam shared in Eve's disobedience or guilt. In this behavior, we have a good example of woman's impetus or force and man's tendency or wish to follow woman wherever she leads, even into evil and death.

Both Adam and Eve hid from the presence of God after eating the forbidden fruit, for they knew they had committed wrong. Later, when Eve told God that "the serpent deceived me, and I did eat", she manifested the natural inclination of a woman to blame, not herself for her wrongdoings, but those around her. Eve completely failed to remember that the Lord God Himself instructed her and her better-half Adam from the very beginning they were put into the garden, not to touch or to eat the forbidden fruit, before her destructive encounter with the serpent. She also refused to accept that she was the one who beguiled her partner Adam to taste the forbidden fruit, which resulted in their fall into sin. The Lord said to the woman, "you will suffer terribly when you give birth. But you will still desire your husband and he will rule over you". (Genesis 3:16 CEV)

In the beginning, it was not the will of God to let man rule over woman, because he created them equally and with the same authority. However, when Eve listened to the serpent and grossly disobeyed God, He immediately enacted or created a new law for man to rule over his wife (his own bones and flesh). This enactment by God likewise the curse of both the serpent and man has never been changed till this time. It is the duty of the woman to always be humble, to serve and to respect her husband, from whom she was created. The man also should respect, help and love the wife as much as he loves himself. (Ephesians 5:33) The basis of a sound balanced relationship of giving and receiving.

As a result of their disobedience, Eve and her partner Adam immensely lost their glorious "paradise" with pain. When the couple had their God-given children, it was there Eve experienced all the pains of childbirth, never forgetting what the Lord God told her when they sinned in the garden, "I will multiply your pain in childbirth". Adam and Eve knew that their children were gifts from God and a joy. However, it did not diminish their pain in fact, they suffered pain when their first son Cain brutally killed his younger brother Abel out of sheer jealousy.

From the beginning, Eve was meant to have children to fulfill the plan of God. Eve became the first woman to speak with God, the first sinner, the first to feel pain in childbirth, and to shed tears of sorrow in witness to the experience of death of a loved one.

"I will put enmity between thee and the woman, and between thy seed and her seed, it shall bruise thy head, and thou shalt bruise his heel". (Genesis 3:15)

By the grace and mercy of God, Eve was the first woman to whom the future salvation after the fall of man was promised. Afterwards she gave birth to her third son who was named Seth. The meaning of the child's name was "to establish" or "to appoint" and he was the strongest of her children. Adam and Eve lived on in their son Seth because in the line of Seth's siblings, his son Enosh's descendants started to worship and call upon the name of the Lord. Also the ancestry of Jesus Christ "The Messiah" was to be traced back through the line of Seth.

In spite of Eve's sins and trials as woman, she still stands forward as the great black and the most beautiful mother of all human life through whom also the paradise lost will be perfectly regained.

The Disobedience & The Promise

The betrayal that Adam and Eve committed in the 'Garden of Eden' that day, set off a reprisal that changed the earth bound conditions for man as God intended, for hundreds of thousands of years. The story of man's life upon earth unfolds when the serpent told Eve that she would know good and evil as God knew it and not die. She believed the serpent over the Word of God, perhaps this was her motivation, to know more than what God had intended. She unknowingly risked the loss of her very soul. God's immediate reaction to their betrayal provoked Him to shed the blood of an innocent animal and cover the nakedness of Adam and Eve with animal skins.

Eve's direct disobedience wrought a continuum of future downfalls for all of mankind in the form of sin. Their disobedience resulted in a punishment, ordained by the word of God, bequeathed to Adam and Eve and all humankind. He ordained women's pain through childbirth, men had to toil the soil in hard labor to support himself and his family, and the serpent was to crawl upon its belly all the days of its life. The 'Word' was released for the redemption of man's act for his betrayal to God in the form of judgment. This was bestowed upon the future Son of Man, in the form of prophesies throughout the Old Testament, and realized in the New Testament through his death, rise from the dead as Our Savior, Christ Jesus.

After He clothed Adam and Eve, the story surrounding their life tapers off. However, if we are allowed to read in between the story lines, then we are able to infer into the lives of Adam and Eve; from what is not written about how they adapted to their new surroundings and aforementioned conditions, as human beings upon earth.

After they left the 'Garden of Eden' the next time you read about Eve, specifically, the Bible references her birthing Cain and saying 'God gave me a man.' It leaves us to wonder; were Eve's initial childbearing pains from Cain and then Able and her other children so severe that she cries out to the heavens, each time she gives birth, 'God forgive me.' Adam may have fallen to his knees crying out to God for mercy, upon seeing Eve go through such pain. Maybe Eve felt so remorseful of her disobedience to God that she suffered through her birthing pain quietly, welcoming her suffering because she was burdened with guilt and knew she deserved it. "God gave me a man!" Maybe these were words of hope; a spirited belief that came from her lips that God's forgiveness was on its way. However, the murderous act of Cain upon his brother Able probably added to their pain as parents.

Did Eve feel a stabbing pain of remorse whenever she watched Adam perform exhaustive hard labor as he toiled the soil and returned home to her daily with cuts, bruises and severely exhausted. Did his pain serve as a constant reminder of their disobedience to God? Did she and Adam sit together and reminiscense about the 'Garden of Eden' and how things were made so perfect for their life's existence. Did they cry together as they continued to worship our God, and pray for mercy and forgiveness? Adam and Eve for their disobedience probably suffered great remorse and guilt for their sin. However unbearable their suffering was over what they had thrown away, because of their disobedience, the Bible does not say, so we cannot say. However, what is certain is that in the beginning, biblical references of women in the Bible were minimal. Nonetheless, the character and abilities as well as disabilities of women are born through the actions of Eve.

Thereafter, it appears as if Eve performed her womanly duties and roles as wife, mother, grandparent and great grandparent as they continued to populate the earth. Eve nurtured her many children, and was a helpmate, a strong backbone to her husband as God ordained. He blessed them, with the birth of Seth, their third son. It was Seth's grandson, Enosh that began to physically and emotionally honor God; and He accepted the honor. He did not allow them to die without allowing them to birth a son that would show Him honor with truth, love, and respect as they once did; because they wanted to, not because they felt they had to because of their sin. God's Will is done here through an act of mercy with infinite love. By God shedding the blood of an innocent animal and then using the skin of that animal to cover their nakedness; bequeathing mercy, forgiveness, and love through a promise of a Savior. Man's sin birthed a redeemer, namely Jesus Christ as our Savior, Amen.

Chapter Three

The Story of HAGAR

One will definitely find it very difficult to know, understand, and write well about the general character of Hagar without making reference to some of the historical events of both Abraham and his wife Sarah. Before we deal with the topic, let us first examine carefully the following scriptures in the book of Genesis.

"The crops failed, and there was no food anywhere in the land. So Abraham and his wife Sarai went to live in Egypt for a while. But just before they got there, he said, "Sarai, you are really beautiful! When the Egyptians see how lovely you are, they will murder me because I am your husband. But they won't kill you. Please save my life by saying that you are my sister." As soon as Abraham and Sarai arrived in Egypt, the Egyptians noticed how beautiful she was. The king's officials told him about her and she was taken to his house. The king was good to Abram because of Sarai and Abram was given sheep, cattle, donkeys, slaves (menservants and maidservants) and camels. Because of Sarai, the Lord struck the king and everyone in his palace with terrible diseases. Finally, the king sent for Abram and said to him, "What have you done to me? Why didn't you tell me Sarai was your wife? Why did you made me believe she was your sister? Now I have married her. Take her and go! She's your wife." So the king told his men to let Abram and Sarai take their possession and leave. (Genesis 12:10-20 CEV)

Hagar means flight or escape. She was one of the black young Egyptian maids from the house of the renowned Pharaoh of Egypt. Hagar was given to Abraham's wife Sarah as a maidservant. Many people, after reading the story about Hagar in the Bible, may form a general picture in their minds of her as an African white slave woman from Egypt, whom was typically unkind, proud, disrespectful and ungodly. This preconception about Hagar is only correct physically, but from the religious point of view it is completely wrong.

When we patiently look at the scriptures specifically, we will come to the conclusion that, Sarah's maid Hagar was never a bought slave as others claim, but rather a young and beautiful black Egyptian woman who was given to Sarah as a maid servant, along with other black men and women servants, livestock, silver, and gold. It was a gesture by the then great Pharaoh, who wanted to marry Sarah when Abraham had journeyed to Egypt to make it his home because of the terrible famine, which came upon the land of Canaan.

According to legend, Hagar was one of Pharaoh's daughters. She was then considered a princess; when she saw the miracles her father wrought on behalf of Sarah and her husband Abraham because of the God they served, she said to herself, I would rather be a maid in their house than a mistress in my own home. She voluntarily chose to leave Pharaoh's palaces and joined Abraham and Sarah as they were leaving Egypt for Canaan. Hagar considered Abraham's house as a holy and a righteous place. Unknowingly to Hagar, her future would unfold and reveal that she would bear and nurture her children well.

God called Abraham, as a prophet and the father of many nations. (Genesis 18:18; 20:7) In Abraham's time, every head or father of a large family was considered as a "patriarch" or a "chief." Therefore, Abraham was called a prophet because of his relationship with the Holy God. He was also a patriarch or chief of a great spiritual family or nation.

As a result of Abraham's position, Sarah as his wife is considered a prophetess. (Genesis 11:29; 12:5) Her piety, reveres her as a queen, as his sister she would be a princess. (Genesis 20:12) For this reason, Pharaoh was right to give some men and women servants to both Abraham and Sarah to serve them in all their endeavors. It was their custom or the culture of the land that was demanded in those days.

The Holy Scriptures reveals that Sarah was very industrious, beautiful and religious woman, (Genesis 12:14-16; 20:2) Hence, emotionally, psychologically and spiritually, Sarah saw some good qualities in Hagar after she had been living in her and Abraham's home for more than ten years as a maid. Amongst all the bondwomen who Sarah had in their large family, she found Hagar to be the most hardworking, sincere, respectful, cute, neat, good-spirited and presentable. Hagar eventually became the apple of her eye, and Sarah chose her as a mate to bear a child for her God-fearing, renowned and handsome husband. Sarah did not choose young Hagar by mistake. In other words, Sarah tried Hagar, and found that she had the necessary qualification. Yes, the dark beautiful and young woman was capable, obedient and trustworthy. Now, let us ask ourselves a question, why a maid of such quality would become so arrogant and hateful to her dear mistress Sarah? We are able to see some moral and spiritual reasons for Hagar's thwarted behavior towards Sarah, and so the story continues to unfold.

First, the Lord God had promised Abraham that, He will make him the father of many nations. He will bless him, make his name very great and he will also be a blessing to others. (Genesis 12:2-3) This was a promise by covenant that should not be broken by either God or Abraham and his household. Many years had past since the Lord God had given His promise to Abraham and Sarah to bless them both with a son. Impatience was settling upon them.

"Now Sarai Abram's wife bare him no children and she had an Egyptian handmaid, whose name was Hagar. And Sarai said unto Abram, behold now, the Lord hath restrained me from bearing: I pray thee, go in unto my maid; it may be that I may obtain children by her. And Abram hearken to the voice of Sarai." (Genesis 16:1-6)

From the records of the Holy Scriptures, we have again been informed that, Hagar was purely a black young woman from the ancient and famous city of Egypt in Africa. This was clearly explained in the previous chapter. We also studied that, in the past, black or dark people densely populated Egypt, Ethiopia, Canaan, Libya, Assyria and Babylon before the invasions and conquests by notorious foreigners, from Asia and Eastern Europe. It was revealed that Hagar was a handmaid of Sarah, the legitimate wife of Abraham.

In the eyes of Abraham and Sarah, the promise from God of a child was overdue. Yet, there was no need for pious Sarah's impatience to belittle or doubt the power and the word of God by directing Abraham, the father of faith to sleep with her maid Hagar in an effort to bear a child. That was Sarah's first unwise decision and fault. The Bible says, "For a thousand years in thy sight are but as yesterday when it is past, and a watch in the night." (Psalm 90:4)

Although Hagar was Sarah's maid, it was totally wrong for Sarah to use Hagar in this way, and without her knowledge or agreement. Abraham and Sarah had no right to arrange to conceive a child through Hagar and ignore the promise that God made to them. Here, Sarah was not as faithful in her belief of God's promise of blessing her with a child. Sarah's disobedience is compared her to Eve's disobedience in the Garden of Eden, when she beguiled Adam to taste the forbidden fruit. Eve did not believe God in the Garden of Eden and Sarah did not believe God's promise that she and Abraham would be given a child in their old age. Time may not transcend knowledge but experience does. Eve doubted, or disrespected the promise of God and also provoked Him. Sarah and Abraham showed lack of faith to the God they worshipped and served. However, Sarah and Abraham would also pay for their actions, for what a man sows is what he reaps! (Galatians 6:7).

Abraham showed his pride at having his first handsome loving child at such an old age, with such a young and beautiful maid, pleased him. Unconsciously he gave Hagar and their son Ishmael preferential treatment before the face of his aged wife Sarah. As a result, Hagar took that as an opportunity for her to interrupt Sarah and Abraham's marriage and assume the rights of her mistress and replace the first wife. Therefore, Hagar disregarded her mistress, who had ordered her into the master's bed with impunity. These human feelings that had prompted Hagar in this manner are common feelings that anyone in this position may have felt and acted upon. Sarah feeling the aggression of Hagar in her own home was prompted to approach Abraham. Sarah said to Abraham: "It is all your fault! I gave you my maid woman, but she has been hateful to me ever since she found out she was pregnant. You (Abraham) have done me wrong, and you will have to answer to the Lord for this." (Genesis 16:5)

It is obviously true that Abraham respected Sarah and did what his betterhalf had initially told him to do. But, perhaps, the way Abraham behaved during the pregnancy of Hagar and after the birth of Ishmael may have been what incited young Hagar to begin to show her hate and disrespect for her mistress. The Lord God again promised Abraham that his wife Sarah would have a male child in her old age, Sarah laughed.

"Sarah laughed within herself, saying, after I am waxed old shall I have pleasure, my lord (Abraham) being old also? The Lord asked Abraham, Why did Sarah laugh? Does she doubt that she can have a child in her old age? I am the Lord! There is nothing too hard for me. I will come back next year at the time I promise, and Sarah will already have a son." When questioned, Sarah was so afraid that she lied and said, "I did not laugh."

"Yes, you did!" He answered. Here too, Sarah committed her second fault before the Lord. She doubted and treated God's Word as unimportant. Finally, because of her old age and that of her husband, she grossly lied because she did not believe. (Genesis18:9-15)

It reads, "And Abraham called the name of his son that was born unto him, whom Sarah bare to him, Isaac. And Sarah said, God hath made me to laugh so that all that hear will laugh with me."(Genesis 21:3, 5)

The Spirit of the Lord directed Abraham to name the son born to him by Sarah as Isaac, meaning laughter. Sarah also with the same sprit praised God for giving her husband a son in his old age, and that his name will let every one laugh with her. (Genesis 21:6) Here Sarah realized that, what she one time concealed in her heart and lied about before the Lord, had served as a revelation for her beloved son's name. "The Lord said, "Yes you did laugh." (Genesis 18:15)

It continues, "And the child grew, and was weaned; and Abraham made a great feast the same day that Isaac was weaned. And Sarah saw the son of Hagar the Egyptian, which she had born unto Abraham, mocking. Wherefore she said unto Abraham, cast out this bondwoman and her son: for the son of this bondwoman shall not be heir with my son, even with Isaac." (Genesis 21:8-10).

As a result of Ishmael's mockery, Sarah's anger and harshness grew into such a degree that she ordered her very religious husband to get rid of Hagar and her son. It was a very hard and disturbing action for Abraham to perform. The Holy Scripture confirmed this. And the thing (Sarah's decision) was very grievous in Abraham's sight because of his son. (Genesis 21:11)

Abraham knew for sure that his wife Sarah was instigating him to send the inexperienced Hagar and her child into the waterless desert to die. In fact, Abraham became very confused and did not know what to do until the Lord God Himself intervened to send both Hagar and her son away. (Genesis 16:7-16).

Let us again ask ourselves, what influenced Hagar's child Ishmael to ridicule his mother's mistress and her son Isaac? Sarah entirely forgot the wrongs she did by directing her husband to give Hagar a child. She laughed in her heart about the promise that God reconfirmed and she lied before the Lord for what she had truly did, which later God used to name her son Isaac. As previously mentioned in these writings, our Lord is a true God and all what He does is perfectly right. We can honestly say that, it was the Lord who gave back to Sarah, the fruit from the seed she planted, and it was bitter. That was the results Sarah reaped because of her unbelief and falsehood. There is an old adage that says, "What goes around, comes around."

We should be very sincere to admit that, not all women of our time are like that black and gorgeous Egyptian maid that survived the feeling of being rejected and went away to no where. Like any other human being, if Hagar had shown Sarah the bad side of her character, she had also the good side of her character that admittedly Sarah had seen and liked. From a religious point of view, we can honestly conclude that, whatever wrong Hagar and her son Ishmael did against Sarah and her son Isaac, was placed into motion because of the behavior she displayed towards the Lord God.

Because of Hagar's strong faith, prayer, courage, and affliction, the Lord God promised to bless her son Ishmael to have many descendants, become the father of twelve princes, and make his family a great nation. (Genesis 16:10-12; 21:17-21)

Today, the world needs women whom the Lord sees and says, "Don't be afraid, and live to tell about it."

The Affliction & The Blessing

Sarah, Abraham's wife, a free woman, orchestrated the act between Hagar a bondwoman and her husband that resulted in Hagar birthing a son for Abraham named Ishmael. This is when Hagar's affliction was about to begin. Abraham was an old man at this time and he was proud that he had fathered a child. God had bequeathed that Abraham and Sarah were to be blessed with a son. Sarah had grown old, and it seemed that God's blessing was never going to be realized. Sarah and Abraham were desperate for a child. Therefore, Sarah chose Hagar and requested that Abraham be with her maidservant to father a child. Once Hagar was pregnant with the child, Abraham began to show more favor toward Hagar than his wife Sarah. Hagar began to treat Sarah indifferently as if she, Hagar was the first wife. This disheartened Sarah. She confronted Abraham, reminding him that she allowed him to be with Hagar so that they would have a son through Hagar. Now she was feeling he had changed in the way he was feeling toward the maidservant and the way he was feeling about her.

This was not God's plan, but Sarah and Abraham's act of faithlessness to God's promise had resulted in the birth of Ishmael, Hagar and Abraham's son. God spoke to Sarah and Abraham again and reminded them of His promise to give them a son. Sarah's heart still reflected her disbelief and she laughed at the thought of having a child at her age. But, God's Will was done and Isaac was born to Sarah and Abraham.

Hagar was young and beautiful and thrived for the attentions of her son's father, Abraham. Hagar began to make use of, and impose her womanly charm toward Abraham, disregarding and disrespecting Sarah. Ishmael had mocked Sarah and his younger brother Isaac. Sarah continued to cry to Abraham for him to send Hagar and her son Ishmael away. Sarah's heart was heavy with the problem she had caused because of her unfaithfulness. Hagar was intentionally reminding Sarah of her youngness and her beauty. Hagar's youth and beauty was a constant reminder to Sarah that her own beauty was fading due to age. Abraham had mixed emotions about what to do in this emotionally and depressing situation.

God showed Sarah mercy; Abraham was obedient to God and obeyed His instruction to send Hagar and his first-born son away. Hagar (a gentile) pondered the wrong that she felt had been done to her by her mistress. She had Abraham's first son, surely she was more than a maidservant, more beautiful. She had attempted to run away before to relieve her anxiety and frustration of the situation, but now Abraham was sending her away. How could she bare such rejection from the father of Ishmael. She had left her land and her family because she had felt spiritually pulled to be a part of Abraham's household. Now she was being asked to leave and she felt devastated.

God promised Hagar that Ishmael the son of Abraham would be blessed. Hagar was a strong woman and mother. She survived life's trials and tribulations with God's blessing. Ishmael did receive God's blessing and his descendants were a great nation. However, Ishmael was born of the flesh, from Hagar a slave woman, and Isaac was ordained to be born as

God's promise to Abraham and Sarah, born of His Spirit. It is through the spirit, the prevailing word of God, that we are in faith allowed to share in the inheritance and acceptable to God in spirit, a child of the free woman, not the bondwoman. God's Will is done. (Galatians 4:28-31)

Chapter Four

The Story of KETURAH

Not much is written about Abraham's beautiful wife Keturah in the Holy Scriptures. The Bible only mentions the name of her husband, her great children and her descendants. However, her story is quite different from that of Abraham's former two wives, Sarah, and Hagar.

Keturah means a sweet smelling substance or incense. The scripture explains that after the death of his legitimate and blessed wife Sarah, that Abraham the father of the faithful, and the friend of the Lord God, after his mourning married again.

"When Sarah was one hundred twenty-seven years old, she died in Kiriath-Arba, better known as Hebron, in the land of Canaan. After Abraham had mourned for her, he went to the Hittites and said, "I live as a foreigner in your land, and I don't own any property where I can bury my wife. Please let me buy a piece of land." (Genesis 23:1-4 CEV)

Abraham decided to have another wife because of his divine responsibilities to the Lord God and his people. The scriptures explain that, after the death of Sarah and during Abraham's old age, he married Keturah. She was younger and the most humble of Abraham's wives. They took their vows in Hebron the land of Canaan. Keturah became the third wife of Abraham. She was the epitome of joy and peace in Abraham's life.

"Then again Abraham took a wife, and her name was Keturah, descendant of Nimrod. And she bares him Zimran, and Jokshan, and Medan, and Midian, and Ishbak and Shuah. And Jokshan begot Sheba, and Dedan, And the sons of Dedan, were Asshurim, and Letushim, and Leummim. And the sons of Midian; Ephah, and Epher, and Hanoch, and Abidah, and Edaah. All these were the children of Keturah." (Genesis 25:1-4)

In an attempt to research the nationality or legacy of Keturah, it is significant to explain that the city of Hebron where Keturah and Abraham was married was inhabited and owned by the Hittites, the descendants of the son of Canaan called Heth.

Although the scriptures do not name the parents, nation, race, or legend of Keturah, history reveals her as the third and last wife of the faithful father of the world Abraham, the daughter or descendant of the Black great leader Nimrod of Ethiopia (Africa) in the Bible.

Nimrod was the mighty hunter before the Lord. It is also referenced that, Abraham was twice given maidservants as a gift by both the great Pharaoh of Egypt and King Abimelech of Gerar, for their big mistake to take Sarah as a wife, because of Abraham's deceit, when he visited their land as a foreigner. We are stating that, the then maidservant, Keturah, may have come from either Egypt in Africa or Gerar in Canaan. Making it possible that, Keturah as a beautiful young 'black' Hittite woman and her people were from Gerar and Hebron who were brethren or descendants of the powerful Canaanites were also black people that migrated from Africa.

It is a fact, that the daily responsibility of Abraham to God as a prophet, and the responsibilities to his nation, as a patriarch, gradually changed the life of this young and very self-disciplined maid Keturah. To be the partner, a wife of such a great man as Abraham, Keturah became god-fearing, industrious, serious, intelligent, hospitable and respectful. The miracles that the Lord God wrought on behalf of Keturah's husband Abraham made Keturah feel secure, humble, and more faithful. She developed spiritually and always had peace of mind to encourage and to comfort her generous and religious husband. She was very fertile and had no rival for her husband's affection during her time with Abraham. There was no chance of repeating the ill regard that had come between Sarah and her maid Hagar.

Apart from her inner qualities, Keturah was a woman whom Abraham had more joy, comfort, and peace of mind with, during his extended life's blessings, and great achievements on earth. Keturah's character proved to be compatible and favorable to Abraham. The old African Adage, that says, "the precious and expensive beads do not make noise" can be referred to the relationship between Keturah and Abraham. Never in Keturah's story does she trouble Abraham to feel disturbed or sad in his heart. The success of a nation begins in the heart of its people, and Abraham was very happy and so were his people.

Keturah married Abraham after he had fully received his blessings that the Lord God intended to give to him from the time he was called. She was also spiritually blessed as Abraham's wife. She adored Abraham and his ways became her ways. Keturah and her husband Abraham had six great princes and two wonderful grandsons that she nurtured and reared with the love of God in her heart. Out of these grandsons came the powerful Midianite race. She became the mother of the Midianites who were one of the races of the Canaanites. She was also considered a famous woman in her time by bringing together and supporting her two stepsons Isaac and Ishmael as they buried their beloved father Abraham, the most blessed, faithful and a friend of God, in peace. (Genesis 25:8&9)

Finally, Keturah's inner spirit and independent love for God had evolved. Her general character reflected her charm, graciousness, inner spiritual beauty and strength as a wife and a nurturing mother of the blessed Midianite race.

Joy and Peace

God blessed Abraham with a younger wife namely Keturah after Abraham's first wife Sarah died at 127 years old. She was Abraham's soul mate. We can only imagine Abraham's feeling of sorrow upon her death. However, it is not so important that we empathize with Abraham's feelings over Sarah's demise, because death is merely the end process of our flesh, our carnal life, and the beginning of a spirited full eternal life, as ordained by God, should one choose.

Keturah a gentile from the land of Canaan, was called by God to help Abraham continue the fulfillment of a covenant that He had with Abraham. Her role was clearly to be a helpmate to Abraham and have his children. She was young, wise, strong, obedient, loving, trustworthy and a supportive wife. She was soft spoken and yielded to Abraham's needs. She had his children and nurtured them, fulfilling God's directive to Eve, meant for all women; strengthen your husband and bear his children. Keturah and Abraham's life together was bound in joy and peace as they fulfilled their Godly mission, bringing forth the reality of God's promise, that Abraham will be recognized as the father of all nations, and his seeds will be blessed.

Upon her husbands demise, Keturah as the mother of the Midianite race in her wisdom and with love extended honor to Abraham's eldest sons, Isaac the child of the free woman and Ishmael the child of the bondwoman. Keturah called them to tend the burial ceremony of their father and stand together in honor. They stood with Abraham and Keturah's six sons and grandsons, in heartfelt ceremony, as they all honored their father's life as a friend of God, an obedient prophet as their father, the father of all nations was placed to rest, Abraham! So Keturah as a third wife is named in the ancestry of Jesus Christ, the Will of God is done!!

Chapter Five

The Story of TAMAR

The name Tamar means Palm-tree. The record of Genesis tells us very little about Judah's former daughter-in-law, excluding where she came from and her parents.

As we reference the Holy Scripture in telling the Story of Tamar, we find that Judah left his other brothers and went on a journey to marry the daughter of a certain Canaanite named Shuah. Tamar was also a Canaanite woman that Judah married for his first son Er while in this foreign land. These Canaanites were the descendants of Canaan, the fourth son of Ham who was the father of all the "Black" or "Hamitic" races.

The Bible says, "And Judah took a wife for Er his firstborn, whose name was Tamar. And Er, Judah's firstborn, was wicked in the sight of the Lord; and the Lord slew him.

And Judah said unto Onan, go in unto thy brother's wife, and marry her, and raise up seed to thy brother. And Onan knew that the seed should not be his; and it came to pass, when he went in unto his brother's wife, that he spilled it on the ground, lest that he should give seed to his brother. And the thing, which he did, displeased the Lord: wherefore He slew him also." (Genesis 38:6-10).

As a result of the wickedness of the two sons of Judah, Er and Onan, God killed them, leaving Judah one remaining son Shelah, the youngest. Instead of Judah sincerely recognizing the sin of his sons, he blamed Tamar in his heart for being the cause of his sons' death. Judah maliciously thought that, his daughter-in-law Tamar possessed with an evil spirit that killed his two obstinate sons. Tamar was shamed because of Judah's ungodly belief that she was the reason his sons had died and for being a woman with a barren womb.

Then said Judah to Tamar his daughter-in-law, remain a widow at thy father's house until Shelah my son be grown: for he said, lest peradventure he die also, as his brethren. And Tamar went and dwell in her father's house." (Genesis 38:11).

Judah falsely promised that when Shelah grew up that he would marry Tamar. He intentionally deceived Tamar because he did not want the same thing to happen to his third and last son Shelah, that happened to his other two sons. Tamar's intuition was that her father-in-law Judah, would not honor his promise and give her Shelah his youngest son to marry, after losing his two former precious sons. Tamar also thought that if Judah did honor his claim, that maybe he was right that what had occurred to his two brothers, would happen to Shelah. However, the love of having offspring or children was very much in Tamar's heart. For this reason, she was forced or obsessed with having children. So she wrought a plan of how she might seek her right to motherhood from her father-in -law Judah. Since Judah had discretely intended to deny Tamar his third son Shelah, Tamar thought of a way to force Judah to accept and honor his duty as promised to her under the Levirate law.

The cunning Tamar heard that, her father-in-law Judah was reading to take a trip to be in the hills of Timnath with his friend Hirah, the Adullamite, to shear his sheep because it was sheep-shearing season. Tamar's impatience would not allow her to remain clean or pure any longer for the time it would take

Shelah to grow up and give her a child. She decided to dress in something other than her widow's clothes and to cover her face with a veil. Tamar sat outside the town of Enaim on the road to Timnath, where she knew her father-in-law had to pass. When her father-in-law Judah came by and saw her, he thought she was a prostitute. He gave Tamar a proposition and they agreed to terms. He had sexual intercourse with her, which resulted in Tamar becoming pregnant. Although she presented herself as a prostitute to attract Judah's attention, she was not a prostitute as people today may think. She was rather a self-respecting, clever, humble woman, determined to deceive or outsmart Judah and satisfy her right to bear children and have succession, according to the Laws during that time.

"When Judah saw her, he thought her to be a harlot; because she had covered her face. And he turned unto her by the way, and said, go to, I pray thee, let me come in unto thee (for he knew not that she was his daughter-in-law). And she said, what wilt thou give me, that thou mayest come in unto me? And he said; I will send thee a kid from the flock. And she said, Wilt thou give me pledge, till thou send it? And he said, what pledge shall I give thee? And he said, thy signet, and thy bracelets, and thy staff that is in thine hand. And he gave it to her, and came in unto her, and she conceived by him. And she arose, and went away, and laid by her veil from her, and put on the garments of her widowhood." (Genesis 38:15-19)

About three months later, Judah was told that his daughter-in-law Tamar was pregnant by whoredom. He became very angry about this report, and immediately ordered that Tamar be brought forth and burned. However, when Tamar came before Judah holding his signet, bracelets and staff, she had requested he give her. She said to Judah, "discern, I pray thee, whose are these?

The scripture reads, "And Judah acknowledged them, and said, She hath been more righteous than I: because that I gave her not to Shelah my son. And he knew her again no more." (Genesis 38:25-26).

Judah could not deny their ownership and honestly admitted that they were his. The final statement by Judah proved that, Tamar was not an unclean woman. However, the whole guilt or wrong was with her father-in-law Judah.

Initially, as with every human being, Judah might have been offended and angry to think that, he had been deluded into having sex with his daughter-in-law. However, according to the Levirate Law of the past, Tamar did nothing evil before God and the people. In fact, Tamar did more justice to herself in many ways while making certain that the family line of her father-in-law Judah be continued, through himself, not through his three sons Er, Onan or Shelah.

Judah could not kill the woman who courageously and intelligently helped to continue his family line, since that was what he, Judah wanted from the beginning when he brought Tamar for his son Er. What was first considered as a deceit and evil on the part of the Canaanite woman Tamar, at last was accepted and respected as the truth and a blessing on the part of the Jewish man Judah.

When the beautiful and young Tamar was in labor and it was determined that she was carrying twins, a hand emerged, when the hand emerged from Tamar's womb, the midwife tied a red cord about the wrist, but the baby with the red cord was delivered last, which means first was last and last was first. (Mark 10:31; Matthew 20:16) This paradox represents Judah's fateful relation with Tamar. Thus, Judah was first as the father-in-law of the slain boys Er and Onan, and last as the father of their twins Pharez and Zarah. One of the twins namely Pharez, is the grandfather of King David an ancestor of Jesus Christ.

Tamar was one of the most practical, faithful, and courageous woman the world has witnessed. Today, we eagerly need women of Tamar's caliber who would be more righteous than men. Lastly, the legality and courage of Tamar's effort made her like a Palm tree whose leaves will never wither in the tribe of Judah.

A Rite to Motherhood

Tamar husband's culture dictates that when a woman marries into a family, she is to care for her husband and birth his children. Tamar's husband had died before she could conceive a child. The custom of her husband's and her father-in-law Judah's culture is that the responsibility of a deceased relatives widow is to be cared for by another living relative in every way. In compliance with tradition, Judah promised Tamar that his other son Onan would take the place of her deceased husband Er and give her a child. However, he spilled his seed on the ground and was killed because God was dissatisfied by his action. Judah promised Tamar that his younger son Shelah would take the place of her deceased husband and give her a child when he arrived of age. Judah was confused as to the reasoning behind the death of his two sons and the part that this woman Tamar may have played in their death. He feared that the life of his younger son might be at stake and had no intention of honoring his promise. Tamar's womanly intuitiveness, allowed her to foresee that Judah would not keep his promise. Tamar's desire to have a child intensified; she felt no kinship from the kinsman of her late husband's people. They looked upon her as a widow without a child, she felt alone.

Tamar knew of Judah's fears to honor his promise and decided to disguise herself as a whore and seduce her father-in-law to lay with her and impregnate her. As outlined in biblical history, the birth of these twins supersedes Tamar's motivation to just have a child. She may have felt that she would be accepted amongst her fellow tribesman, that the birth protected her image or reputation. This may have satisfied her inner emotional desire to become a mother, it certainly ushered her into the family lineage of our Lord Jesus Christ. However, regardless of Tamar's reasons for pursuing Judah to impregnate her, it is God's will that was done, through the birthing of Tamar and Judah's twins Pharez and Zarah. Pharez the oldest son of Judah and Tamar, through his children was born David, the King of Israel. Tamar's rite to motherhood appears to be used righteously to help bring forth a king of God's choosing, thereby meaning that she was motivated by God and obedient to God's will. Knowingly or unknowingly Tamar was used as a vessel for God's greater glory and ultimate plan for mankind upon earth to prevail.

Chapter Six

The Story of ASENATH

Scripture again reports very little about another great African woman. Yet, the meaning of her name is Asenath, her general behavior and her unprecedented involvement in the life of her husband Joseph, indicated that she was very devoted and faithful. Asenath also dedicated her life to both the service of the Lord God and to her nation. Apart from that, she always assisted and encouraged her beloved Hebrew and god-fearing husband.

Asenath means devoted or dedication. She was an Egyptian young and beautiful woman who was happily married to her Hebrew, religious and dream interpreter husband Joseph. Her father's name was Potiphera, a high priest in the city of Heliopolis in Egypt.

"And Pharaoh called Joseph's name Zaphnath-paaneah; and he gave him to wife Asenath the daughter of Potipherah priest of On. Joseph was thirty years old when he stood before Pharaoh King of Egypt. And Joseph went out from the presence of Pharaoh, and went throughout all the land of Egypt. (Genesis 41:45-46).

Asenath was especially chosen by King Pharaoh to marry Joseph. She was probably one of the most beautiful, humble, religious and hardworking Egyptian women at the time of Israelites exodus to Egypt. One cannot write very well about the Egyptian woman Asenath without making reference to the biblical story about her Hebrew husband and dreams interpreter Joseph.

Let us first begin with Joseph's encounter between him and his other brothers. The Word of God revealed that, out of sheer jealousy, young Joseph was sold to Egypt as a slave by his own brothers, and wickedly deceived their aged father Jacob that, some wild animal had eaten him up in the wilderness. (Genesis 37:19-36)

"And it came to pass after these things, that his master's wife cast her eyes upon Joseph, (because the Lord was with him, and he was well built and handsome) and she said, lie with me. But he refused, and said unto his master's wife:

"Behold, my master wotteth not what is with me in the house, and he hath committed all that he hath to my hand; There is none greater in this house than I; neither hath he kept anything from me but thee, because thou art his wife: how then can I do this great wickedness, and sin against God." (Genesis 39:7-9).

Later, Joseph was imprisoned after the wife of his Egyptian master Potiphar falsely accused him of rape. By God's grace and power Joseph was freed when a former prisoner suggested that, Joseph could interpret the Pharaoh's dreams, which he did and finally saved both Egypt and the then world including the Israelites, from a severe or terrible famine. The severity of the said famine drove his brothers to seek urgent assistance from the African famous Pharaoh or Emperor of Egypt and also united them with their brother Joseph that they had sold into slavery.

From experience and so far as the Holy Scriptures are concerned, it was not the custom in the biblical times for Bible writers to focus much attention on women's activities. However, the character of faith, responsibility and the enormous achievement of Asenath's beloved and renowned husband Joseph went a long way in determining Asenath's committed work, support, and encouragement and sacrifice rendered to Joseph, her nation, and God of both Israel and the whole world. The truth is that, Asenath being the daughter of a high priest in Egypt was afforded opportunities that helped build in her good and religious character that was used effectively to support her young intelligent husband Joseph, her children, and her nation Egypt before and after the great famine that visited the land.

The scriptures teach us that, during the severe famine, Joseph met his family because of their need to visit Egypt for supplies. Joseph's brothers made several visits to him and his dear wife Asenath in Egypt to buy food in order to help their large family survive in Canaan. It further explains that, finally, the entire family in Canaan including Jacob and his wives moved to stay in Egypt, after Joseph made himself known to his eleven brothers, that he was Joseph the one they had sold.

Joseph's brothers went down to buy corn in Egypt. And Joseph saw his brethren, and he knew them, but made himself strange unto them; and he roughly said unto them; whence come ye? And they said, from the land of Cannan to buy food."-And Jacob rose from Beersheba and the sons of Israel carried Jacob their father, and their little ones, and their wives, in the wagon, which Pharaoh had sent to carry him. And they took their cattle, and their goods, which they had gotten in the land of Canaan, and came into Egypt, Jacob, and all his seed with him." (Genesis 42:2,3; 46:5-6).

The young Asenath served Joseph's brothers during their various visits to buy corn. She also served his entire family when they finally arrived in the Land of Egypt. She showed reverence, enthusiasm, eagerness and readiness towards responding to the intense and double responsibilities placed before her regarding her husband's large family from Canaan and her onerous duties to the nation of Egypt in general. She developed working tools to enhance her effectiveness. This led her to be more tactful, smart, hardworking, respectful, hospitable and humble, even in moments of trial or adversity.

Asenath recognized the blessing that God had bestowed upon her as the wife of Joseph. She realized that she may have never met him or married Joseph if it were not for the jealous act his brothers committed. Not only was she grateful but Joseph' life had excelled to the glory of God. That which was meant for Joseph's bad turned out for his greater good and she Asenath was chosen to be a part of the blessing.

Asenath worked diligently showing her gratitude toward the life she was chosen to lead. Surely his family could see the blessings that had been bestowed upon Joseph. Asenath's unspeakable beauty and sound diplomacy in dealing with both private and public matters made her very noble and more protective of her handsome husband Joseph and her children. She was Joseph's backbone and greatly influenced her industrious husband while he reigned as governor or prime minister of the great and civilized empire of Egypt, and as the leader and spokesman for his large Hebrew family.

The pious Asenath gave birth to two famous ancestors of our Lord Jesus Christ named Manasseh and Ephriam. Joseph the Hebrew and dreamer became a dynamic prime minister of the Coptic Land (Egypt), a very successful and respectful leader among his brothers with many descendants like a fruitful vine near a stream. Then, there had to have been an Egyptian wife and lovely mother supporting him. This God-fearing African daughter Asenath chose to live up to her precious name and great nation.

Dedication

Asenath a Black Egyptian women loved her husband and was dedicated to fulfilling duties that would promote her and her families independence and respect throughout their community. As Joseph's wife, Asenath's spiritual essence drove her to be diligent in helping her husband's family. Once she learned that his brothers had sold Joseph to get rid of him because of their petty jealousy, she was even more energetic in serving them. Asenath's understood the blessings that God had bestowed upon Joseph and she was included to take part in it. She was thankful and showed her gratitude to the glory of the Lord. Respectfully, Asenath's life reflected the victory that Joseph had over his brothers that sold him into slavery, and Asenath's intuitiveness knew this. His family now sought Joseph's attention for help. Being a supportive, caring, loving, strong, and righteous wife to Joseph; displaying overwhelming kindness and showing how well he had done for himself, despite the unbelievable deed they had done to him because of their jealousy and treachery, Joseph and his wife Asenath humbly helped them.

Asenath's role as a wife is revealed in the way she went about performing her duties and tasks for God, her family and her nation with love. With regard to Joseph's family as required by God, she outlines the duties of dedication as woman, as a wife, and a mother is to perform for her spiritual growth, to care for her husband, children and family. Joseph was happy with Asenath; he excelled in his tasks, and was able to be a great provider with Asenath as his backbone, his soul mate. Although Pharoah chose Asenath, she was motivated by the will of God to be used as a vessel of dedication, a symbol of the perfect way God intended for man and woman to live and love upon earth.

Chapter Seven

The Story of ZIPPORAH

To effectively portray the story of Zipporah the wife chosen for Moses, we must first introduce the role that Moses was called by God to perform. It is during the time that Moses fled from Egypt after discovering his true Hebrew ancestry that his rightful path was revealed. His heart-felt provocation to murder an Egyptian revealed his rites of passage as a Hebrew and set his feet on a path that embraced his life story, paved by God. The story of Moses has proven to be the greatest story ever told and his wife Zipporah played a significant part in it. Zipporah's part in the life of Moses may appear to be small as it is denoted in the Bible, however, we pray that the Spirit of God will reveal to you this woman's role as meeting the standards of God's request since the time of Adam and Eve.

Zipporah's name means "bird," she was a young Midianite woman whose father was the famous priest of Midian namely Jethro. We would perform a great injustice to Zipporah, if we were only to look at the moral aspect of her character, without looking at the spiritual aspect of it. She was chosen by God to marry Israel's great prophet, lawgiver, and leader, namely Moses.

Midian was the fourth son Abraham fathered with his glorious and peaceful third wife Keturah, after the death of his first blessed wife Sarah. Jethro was a great grandson, of Cush of Ethiopia, the son of the "Black" ancestry, Ham. Zipporah was one of his seven daughters who met Moses in the land of Midian soon after he fled Egypt because of the death he caused to a young Egyptian.

"And it came to pass in those days, when Moses was grown, that he went out unto his brethren, and looked on their burdens; and he spied an Egyptian smiting a Hebrew, one of his brethren. And he looked this way, and that way, and when he saw that there was no man, he slew the Egyptian, and hid him in the sand. And when he went out the second day, behold, two men of the

69

Hebrews strove together: and he said to him that did the wrong, wherefore smitest thou thy fellow?

And he said who made thee a prince and a judge over us? Intendest thou to kill me, as thou killest the Egyptian? And Moses feared, and said, surely this thing is known. Now when Pharaoh heard this thing, he sought to slay Moses. But Moses fled from the face of Pharaoh, and dwelt in the land of Midian; and sat down by a well." (Exodus 2:11-12, 15)

After all the care, good living, comfort, and untold riches Moses found himself in as an adopted child of the princess of Egypt, he ungratefully killed or murdered a young Egyptian and buried him in the bear sand in support of his Hebrew brother. For fear of the sin he committed, Moses had to escape from his comfortable home in Egypt to dwell in the land of Midian as a foreigner.

"Now the priest of Midian had seven daughters: and they came and drew water, and filled the troughs to water their father's flock. And the shepherds came and drove them away: but Moses stood up and helped them, and watered their flock.

Jethro's daughters spoke of the kind and courageous act that Moses had done and Jethro wanted to meet him. "And said unto his daughters, and where is he? Why is it that ye have left the man? Call him, that he may eat bread. And Moses was content to dwell with the man: and he gave Moses Zipporah his daughter." (Exodus 2: 16-17, 20-21)

The Holy scripture explains that, Moses was one day sitting some place by a well, when the priest of Midian namely Jethro's seven daughters came up to water their father's sheep and goats. Some other shepherds tried to drive them away but Moses saw this, so, he came to their rescue and watered their flock for them. When the seven daughters returned home, they immediately reported the incident of what Moses had done for them, to their dear father. Jethro heard about Moses' kindness to his daughters and happily invited him to eat with them in his house. Moses was encouraged to stay with Jethro's family and he finally agreed to stay. Jethro later gave Moses his oldest, pretty, and humble daughter Zipporah to marry.

Before Zipporah was married to Moses, she was already a God-fearing young woman. The reason is that, her beloved father Jethro was a very religious man and also a priest. He influenced the character of his precious daughter. Zipporah was smart, intelligent, respectful, candid, hospitable and the most humble among her sisters in order to have been chosen to marry a spirit-filled, courageous, just, most humble, and great prophet like Moses.

Among the women characters of the Bible, Zipporah had a unique quality that was not found in any one of them, namely her strength and independence. Her dear father had no sons among his children, she automatically became the chief or the leading shepherd girl over her other sisters in the house of their father. Zipporah took on tasks that engaged her to be very responsible and a fair-hearted daughter. She took great care of her father's business with her younger sisters help. As a reliable and honest wife of Israel's famous prophet and leader, she became more industrious, steadfast, diplomatic, dynamic, and a good-spirited woman, wife, mother, daughter, and sister.

There came a time when Moses, who was called by God to the leadership of his own people, became severely sick because he had neglected the sacred duty of circumcision. This lovely Midian wife of Moses was very clever and she used her wisdom and good-natured qualities to assist her husband whenever she saw fit to do so. Her spiritual understanding and belief in God allowed her to recognize the spirit of Moses' illness. She courageously performed a task that was forbidden for women to do at the risk of death. She seized a piece of flint knife that night while her husband was suffering, and circumcised her son to save her beloved husband Moses from dying. It takes a dutiful spirited woman with courage, love, and wisdom and doubtless faith to perform this act for her dear son and her dying husband. Zipporah was well acquainted with the God she and her family served and she would often share stories with Moses about the God she was taught to serve. Jethro was also a teacher that help guide Moses to an understanding about the God he served, and most of all God's choice of Moses to lead his people was a journey of learning, understanding, servitude and faith. Moses learned to love, respect, admire, worship, honor and obey the God he served.

Therefore, it is totally wrong or absurd for people to portray Zipporah as a woman of harsh temper, unsupportive, and less religious. This was the exact mistake or bad criticism made by both Moses' brother Aaron and sister Miriam concerning this Ethiopian (black) woman Zipporah. And as a result of that the Lord God became very angry with them and Miriam, the sister of the Prophet Moses was severely punished and disgraced with leprosy on her skin. (Numbers 12:1-15)

According to scriptures, Zipporah was a woman that was devout in her servitude to her family and her husband Moses. She, along with her two sons, followed Moses every place he went, even before the "Great Pharaoh" of Egypt. Her two great princes she had with Moses were Gershom and Eliezer who were the renowned ancestors of the Lord Jesus Christ. One very important thing, which we should not forget is that Zipporah, as one of the black female widows in the ancient Israel, whom did not see the dead body of her great and beloved husband.

The only conclusion we may quite honestly draw from the whole life of Zipporah is that, she was absolutely the perfect mate for her Israeli husband, leader, and prophet Moses. Her religious uplifting, and unique character was an unfailing symbol of her name "bird."

Wisdom and Service

Zipporah was the oldest of her sisters. She was considered wise, strong and steadfast in her task to protect and serve her family. It was her and her father Jethro that Moses watched and learned from as they worshipped and respected a God that he was beginning to develop a relationship with. God had a master plan and summoned Moses to the burning bush and spoke with him while assigning him the task and journey of a lifetime. God taught Moses and developed a relationship and bond with him, despite Moses' initial unwillingness to accept the task God blessed him with. Zipporah was the wife that understood and supported the journey that Moses was called by God to do. She protected and loved Moses very much. Zipporah was always a strong support for her husband Moses. In her wisdom and spiritual understanding, she assisted Moses by circumcising her son. This prevented God from killing Moses. During that time circumcisions had to be performed, as a religious duty. She understood what was expected of her as Moses helpmate. She performed her wifely, and motherly duties with faithfulness and obedience. Zipporah was quiet woman, a watchful, and obedient wife. She felt honored and grateful that God used her husband, and accepted her role in his life wholeheartedly. God's will is done!

Chapter Eight

The Story of RAHAB

The meaning of Rahab is large. She was a Canaanite woman from the beautiful, prosperous and populated city of Jericho. Jericho was the strongest of the fortified cities of the land of Canaan, also described as "City of Palms." That great and awesome city was surrounded and protected by two strong walls about fifteen feet apart. Jericho was a land flowing with milk and honey and the people were very prosperous too.

"The two spies left the Israelite camp at Acacia (Shittim) and went to Jericho where they decided to spend the night at the house of a prostitute named Rahab. But someone found them and told the king of Jericho, "some Israelites men came here tonight, and they are spies." So the king sent soldiers to Rahab's house to arrest the spies. Meanwhile, Rahab had taken the men up to the flat roof of her house and had hidden them under some piles of flax plants that she had put there to dry. The soldiers came to her door and demanded, "Let us have the men who are staying at your house. They are spies. She answered, "some men did come to my house, but I didn't know where they had come from. They left about sunset, just before it was time to close the town gate. I don't know where they were going, but if you hurry, maybe you can catch them." (Joshua 2:1-6 CEV)

The book of Joshua vividly teaches us how fortified and protected Jericho was with its hardworking, cultured, and rich people. However, the atrocious behavior of the people in the city was abhorrent to the Lord God. And as a result, the Lord turned against them and promised to give that prosperous land to the Israelites through Joshua. Therefore, their Prime Minister Joshua needed the two courageous and intelligent spies to go on a secret mission in Jericho.

The scripture reveals that, Rehab was indeed an experienced harlot. She was probably a prominent and very respectful innkeeper in the eyes of her people. Her pretty and entertaining house occupied a place on the strong wall of Jericho city. For the two spies to avoid identity in entering the gate of Jericho, they swiftly mixed with the crowds outside the city. The advantageous position or location of Rahab's house aided them to hurry into it for protection. She instantly saw the godly and noble appearance of the spies and tried as much as she could to both assist and to protect them. The two spies found at least a degree of safety in this Canaanite woman's house, whose tribesmen or people were considered idolatrous and unclean.

Though, Rahab was a harlot and unclean woman. Yet she had God working in her heart. She had heard more about the mighty God of Abraham, Isaac and Jacob. She had been told about how the Lord dried up the Red Sea for the Israelites to leave Egypt, destroyed the Amorite kings Sihon and Og from the east of Jordan River, and Israel's God who rules heaven and earth. Rahab's courage and cleverness as an experienced prostitute, her hard work and skills as an innkeeper and linen weaver, and her profound love, faith and trust in the Lord God, made her received and protected completely the two men sent from Israel's camp at Acacia by captain Joshua to spy on Jericho.

Apparently, Rahab cleverly lied when both the soldiers and the authorities of Jericho questioned her about the spies who entered her house. She knew definitely why those spies visited the city and why she also protected and assisted them to successfully escape from the hands of the soldiers.

Rahab said, "Please promise me in the Lord's name that you will be as kind to my family as I have been to you. Do something to show that you won't let your people kill my father and mother and my brothers and sisters and their families. "Rahab," the spies answered, "If you keep quiet about what we're doing, we promise to be kind to you when the Lord gives us this land. We pray that the Lord will kill us if we don't keep our promise! (Joshua 2:12-14 CEV).

For the sake of the Lord God, Rahab aided Joshua's two spies and also kept their secret. Yet, she eagerly sought the protection and salvation of her entire family in the city of Jericho. She seriously had in her heart the same faith and divine revelation that both the Apostle Paul and Silas had.

They said, "Believe on the Lord Jesus Christ, and thou shall be saved, and thy house." (Acts 16:31).

Rahab was not only saving herself, but also the welfare of her entire family. Even though Rehab was a pure Canaanite, a gentile, a harlot and unclean, however, she did not allow her questionable behavior to prevent her from fighting to merit God's protection and salvation for herself and her whole family. It is evident that, Rahab was very faithful and courageous to be willing to risk her own life in order to protect and help the enemy's spies, whom she assumed were on a godly mission. Now, we could frankly say that, her faith was living, for it was proved by her good and honest work. If Rahab took that difficult and dangerous task to protect the spies and severely lied to her own soldiers, king, and authorities, it was because she truly believed in God and also knew that she was very secure with the only and everlasting creator of heaven and earth.

The agreement that Rahab had with the two Israeli spies, encouraged her most to hide them among the stalk of flax on her roof-top until the night, when the city gates were closed, and everybody was out of sight, she allowed the messenger to climb down from the outside wall by a strong cord from her window. The two messengers finally escaped peacefully by the assistance of the harlot, despised, and unclean Canaanite woman of Jericho.

Captain Joshua led his men at God's appointed time and severely attacked Jericho. The magnificent and fortified walls around it fell and the city was burning, Rahab and her family including her father and mother departed and were saved from total destruction of their renowned and beautiful city as promised by the two spies of Joshua. Because of Rahab's faith, trust and love of the Almighty God, Israel's Prime Minister Joshua, who was god-fearing and filled with the spirit of wisdom boldly declared, "The city shall be accursed, even it and all that are therein, to the Lord: only Rahab the harlot shall live, she and all that are with her in the house, because she hid the messengers that we sent," (Joshua 6:17). Believing Gods Word and seriously translating it into action saves a lot.

Our Lord Jesus said, "But go ye and learn what that meaneth, I WILL HAVE MERCY, AND NOT SACRIFICE: for I am not come to call the righteous, but sinners to repentance." (Matthew 9:13).

The Lord Jesus clearly explained here that, the motive of his coming into this world, was to save sinners and also include them in God's plan of protection and salvation for all the human race through their belief, active faith and trust in particular, their unconditional love for God in general.

Later, the faithful, courageous, smart, humble and pretty Rahab and her entire family were joined into the fellowship of the Israelites and they became part of them perpetually. She gloriously married one of the princes of Israel named Salmon, who might be one of the two wise messengers sent to Jericho to spy. Rahab and Salmon's well to do and famous son of Israel, namely Boaz married the faithful, pretty and humble widow Ruth, daughter in law of Naomi. Ruth and her rich and respected husband Boaz became the grandparents of the great King David of Israel.

The most interesting and glorious part of Rahab the harlot's story is that, in the list of ancestors of our Lord and Savior Jesus Christ, we proudly discover the name Rahab along with names of the other three gentile "black" and "colored" women called Tamar, Bath-sheba and Ruth. (Matthew 1:2-6) Now we undoubtedly acknowledge that, it is very hard to dispute the ways and the thoughts of our Lord God. (Isaiah 55:8). It is only (the mind of) God who knows why He involved these wonderful gentile women like Rahab in the lives of his chosen and anointed people.

Jesus said, "For the son of man is come to seek and to save that which was lost." (Luke 19:10)

The Lord continues to teach us today and tell us that, He did not come to this world of sin to seek and save those who proudly and hypocritically say they are righteous and have no sin, but to those who are humble and fully accept that they are sinners and need help and forgiveness. The Lord is seriously seeking all the repented people either Jew or Gentile, black or white, rich or poor to bring them into the spirit-filled life of God. (Roman 10:12-13) Condemning the old tradition and self-righteousness of the elders and chief priests; Jesus again said: "Verily I say unto you, that the tax-collectors (publicans) and harlots go into the kingdom before you."(Matthew 21:31)

Rahab the harlot of Jericho put her courage, faith, and love into practice and saved herself and her household from complete destruction. We pray that God's word continues to encourage the courageous and religious women like Rahab, that sincerely protect and assist God's messengers. They quietly nurture what the Lord is doing in their lives and are blessed.

The Faithful

Rahab's kinsman considered her a harlot, but God choose to use her as a human vessel for His will to be done. It was Rahab that had heard stories about the God of Abraham, Isaac and Jacob. She marvelled and favored the stories about the God that loved and honored his people to greatness. The many stories that she had heard made her thirst for more and had changed her harlot's heart into heart of faithful obedience to God. A spiritual seed of belief, respect and love, had been sown in Rahab's heart for the God she had heard so much about. When the Israelites found their way into Jericho and into her home, it is understandable the reasoning and motivation of Rahab to assist the Israelites in their journeys. They required her to betray her own people by keeping quiet of the fact that she was hiding them. She did as they asked; Rahab protected them and sent the soldiers away. She requested that the Israelites in turn, protect her and her family should they return to her city. She had faith that they would keep their word and placed her belief in people she had never met, but had understood that they honored and served a God, that in her felt was magnificent and she loved, honored, and respected.

Rahab had heard that they were of the Israelite tribe of people whose God loved and honored them. She initiated her faith boldly, in this instance based on her inner belief that surely, this God would protect her family and her. God directed the Israelites to Rahab; He knew her and recognized the belief, faith, and admiration she held in her heart for Him. She acted upon her belief with unfailing heart felt courage; she was obedient. She knew that if her betrayal were found out, that it would have resulted in her death and the death of her family. Her faithful action reflected her belief that they would keep their promise, so she hid the Israelites from the soldiers. Although Rahab was considered a gentile, she and her family joined the Israelite tribe. Rahab married an Israelite and was the mother of Boaz. Boaz married Ruth and they were the parents of Obed the grandfather of King David. Rahab's stories behold the essence of worship and honor demanded by the God we serve. With honor and earnestness we step forth in faith and obedience and allow the God of Abraham, Jacob, and Isaac to use whatever means or vessel necessary for His will of perfection to be done. Rahab proved herself worthy to be called a child of God.

Chapter Nine

The Story of DELILAH

We must make reference to the history of Samson, whom was the lover of Delilah that helped his enemies ensnare him, and ultimately take his eyesight. This perfect and full story about this Philistine woman's story of deception cannot be given birth, without first referencing Samson this great Israelite leader.

This story holds a very particular, yet interesting meaning that is a bit different than the stories of the other Black and Colored Women of the Bible. The name Delilah means longing, she was a Philistine woman from the Valley City of Sorek. She was the third Philistine lover of Israel's great judge and leader Samson. She was especially employed by the Philistines to discover the secret of Samson's mysterious great strength. Her lover Samson was the son of a godly man called Manoah from the tribe of Dan.

Philistines were permanent and original dwellers in Philistine in the time of Abraham. They were very wealthy, energetic, and warlike, with many strong cities like Gaza the capital, Ashkelon, Ashdod, Gath and Ekron. They were connected or associated with both Cretans in the East Mediterranean and Caphtorim of Egypt in Africa. The Philistines were either black or colored people. They were also Israel's greatest enemies with many strong leaders and fearful giants like Goliath.

As a result of Israel's disobedience to the Lord God, He allowed the Philistines to rule over all of Israel for a good forty years. Later, the Lord saw the sad plight which His people Israel found themselves in, and thought of providing them a deliverer. The angel of the Lord God approached Manoah and his childless wife, a godly pair, and promised that they would have a son, and he would be there to deliver them out from under the Philistines.

"And the children of Israel did evil again in the sight of the Lord; and the Lord delivered them into the hand of the Philistines forty years. And there was a certain man of Zorah of the family of the Danites, whose name was Manoah; and his wife was barren, and bare not. And the Angel of the Lord appeared unto the woman, and said unto her, behold now, strong desire thou art barren bearest not: but thou shall conceive, and bear a son. Now therefore beware, I pray thee, and drink not wine nor strong drink, and eat not any unclean thing: For lo, thou shalt conceive, and bear a son; and no razor shall come on his head: for the child shall be a Nazarite unto God from the womb: and he shall begin to deliver Israel out of the hand of the Philistines." (Judges 13:1-5)

The angel of the Lord gave them some rules to obey and described the work the promised son would come to do for his people, Israel. The angel seriously warned the wife of Manoah that, from her pregnancy to the glorious birth of the child, she should not taste any wine, beer and eat any food forbidden by God's laws. The angel again said, the child would belong to the Lord from the day he is born. The child's hair must never be cut throughout his life. Finally, he would set Israel free from the Philistines.

Manoah's barren wife gave birth to a son just as the angel of the Lord had promised. She named him Samson, and as he grew up, the Lord God blessed Samson and His Spirit sufficiently took control.

The Holy Scripture says, "and the woman bare a son, and called his name Samson: and the child grew, and the Lord blessed him. And the Spirit of the Lord began to move him at times in the camp of Dan between Zorah and Eshtaol-----." (Judges 13:24-25).

Samson was one of the most distinguished Hebrew judges. With the Spirit of the Lord and blessings upon Samson, he achieved many victories over the Philistines and severely punished them. Hence, they hated him and sought many occasions to kill him.

When Samson became a man, he chose to love and marry a Philestine woman. Despite his parents objection to his decision to marry a Philistine woman of his enemies, from an unclean race, he proudly answered them by saying, "She looks good to me," Get her for me! (Judges 14:3)

Delilah was in fact very gorgeous and smart, and she was the third Philistine woman the renowned Samson fell in love with during his time as a chosen leader of Israel. However, the Philistines planned to destroy Samson through the apple of his eye Delilah. The Philistine rulers secretly went to Delilah and advised her to trick their enemy Samson into telling her what made him so strong and what would make him weak. They offered to pay her a handsome promise of one thousand, one hundred pieces of silver from each ruler.

Delilah was a woman with enormous wisdom, influence and intelligence. She also possessed a strange kind of beauty that easily attracted and made Samson more vulnerable to surrender. "And Delilah said to Samson, tell me, I pray thee, wherein thy great strength lieth, and where with thou mightiest be bound to afflict thee." (Judges 16:6)

Delilah cleverly tricked Samson several times in an effort to learn the secret of his awesome power and strength. Initially, Samson tried his best to lie to Delilah, to frustrate her diabolic plans. Delilah forcing Samson to disclose the secret of his strange strength and Samson giving Delilah different and wrong explanations; it became a vital game between the two of them.

It is assumed that Delilah set a very charming trap. She may have made her home a comfortable place for the mighty and famous Samson to relax and feel safe. It is likely that, she presented her home, as peaceful and enjoyable with all kinds of food that were appetizing to Samson's taste. Delilah's plan was cunning and deceptive, she wanted to make Samson completely forget himself and tell her the secret of his strength. Delilah's behavior was seductive and alluring to Samson, he was receptive to her hypnotic advances. She mislead him to get him to believe that he was the only man on this planet she cared and loved. Therefore, she wanted him to treat her the same, and reveal the deepest secret of his heart to her, as a gesture of their love.

"And she said unto him, how canst thou say I love thee, when thine heart is not with me? Thou hast mocked me these three times, and hast not told me wherein thy great strength lieth. And it came to pass, when she pressed him daily with her words, and urged him so, that his soul was vexed unto death; that he told her all his heart, and said unto her, there hath not come a razor upon mine head, for I have been a Nazarite unto God from my mother's womb: if I be shaven, then my strength will go from me, and I shall become weak, and be like any other man." (Judges 16:15-17).

Finally, in an effort to prove his love for her, Samson confessed to Delilah the secret of his power and unprecedented strength. He revealed that his God-given strength came from the seven locks of his hair. This is really the best example of a woman's alluring strength and ability to push a man to follow a woman wherever she leads, even into danger or to his death. When the charming and deceitful Delilah found that she had succeeded and charmed Samson into revealing the secret of his strength, she made him fall asleep on her cozy knee and he slept deeply. She hurriedly called for a man already hidden somewhere in her house to shave the seven locks from his head. She intentionally awoke Samson and said jokingly to him with a soft and loving voice, "The Philistines be upon thee, Samson." (Judges 16:19-20). He later and sadly found out that, his hair had been cut while he rested and all of his God-given strength had been drained from him.

As a result of Samson's disobedience to the divine Word of God, and his low sense of morals as some people may say, the angry Philistines were able to catch and arrest him. The promise to release Israel from under the grasp of the Philistines appeared to be lost without Samson. They tortured Samson and destroyed his two eyes, finally he was taken to their capital city called Gaza. They put him to work, turning a millstone to grind grain for their food. Fortunately, Samson's hair started to grow again. His marvelous strength also began to grow everyday without the knowledge of the Philistines.

One day the rulers had a big party and made many sacrifices to their god Dragon for delivering Samson, their greatest enemy into their hands. They brought Samson from the prison and made fun of him for a while and told him to stand near the pillars that supported the roof of their gathering house. On that day, the house was full of men and women and also all the rulers of the Philistines were there. And upon the roof of the house, there were about three thousand men and woman.

"And Samson called unto the Lord, and said, O' Lord God, remember me, I pray thee, and strengthen me, I pray thee, only this once, O' God, that I may at once avenge the Philistines for destroying my two eyes. And Samson took hold of the two middle pillars upon which the house stood, and on which it was borne up: one with his right hand, and the other with his left hand. And Samson said, let me die with the Philistines. And he bowed himself with all his might; and the house fell upon the lords, and upon all the people that were therein. So the dead which he slew at his death were more than they which he slew in his life." (Judges 16:28-30)

The final result of Samson's disobedience to God and his surrender of his life to Delilah, caused him to be captured, blinded, and enslaved. He died with the destruction of his enemies, completing his God ordained mission.

Although it was the Philistines that sought to use a woman as the weapon to capture Samson, we are surprised that Samson befell the same weakness of Adam. His feelings for Delilah made him forget his God ordained mission. The Spirit of the Lord was with Samson from birth, yet he chose to marry or make love with women from a tribe who were Israel's number one enemy. Also, Samson as a wise leader and judge of Israel belittled himself and unreasonably surrendered to his first Philistine woman and later to his deceitful and dangerous lover Delilah. The book of Judges chapter fourteen clearly explains the disobedience of Samson, which led him into the beautiful arms of Delilah that resulted in his disastrous demise.

"Then his father and his mother said unto him, is there never a woman among the daughters of thy brethren, or among all my people, that thou goes to take a wife of the uncircumcised Philistines? And Samson said unto his father, get her for me; for she pleaseth me well. "But his father and his mother knew not that it was of the Lord, that he sought an occasion against the Philistines: for at that time the Philistines had dominion over Israel." (Judges 14:3-4).

One vital fact we should not forget is that, Manoah and his barren wife gave birth to Samson to severely punish the Philistines and to finally deliver the Israelites, his people, from their wicked hands. When God revealed the opportunity to Samson to fulfill his mission, God's Will was done. "For my thoughts are not your thoughts, neither are your ways my ways." (Isaiah 55:8) Therefore, if the great Samson of Israel excessively loved and gave too much of his time only to be deluded by Delilah, then it is God's will that allowed this to happen.

Delilah, a Philistine was faithful to her genre and God knew her not, but used her just the same for his greater good to be done. Samson was comfortable with Delilah and enjoyed being in her presence; God placed her as a tool in Samson's path. She assisted Samson in his mission by reminding him that she was a Philistine, willing to destroy him and help blind him and then mock him with her victory. She was used to rectify Samson's behavior in the end. It is because of Delilah that Samson was forced to remember the reason for his birth. This motivated Samson to liberate his people from perpetual slavery and hardships. The Holy Scripture declares: "For man looketh on the outward appearance, but the Lord looketh on the heart." (Samuel 16:7)

It could be that Delilah was the Philistine woman who caused or influenced the words in the book of Micah: "Trust ye not in a friend, put ye not confidence in a guide: keep the door of thy mouth from her that lieth in thy bosom". "A man's enemies are the men of his own house." (Micah 7:5 and 6)

Divinely, we can deduce and conclude that although Delilah unknowingly participated in the destruction of her people, it was the motivation of God which led her to be able to seduce the already flagrant disobedient Samson. Although Delilah was not of the same faith or calling as Samson, but the one and true God sought her and used her for His will to be done. Delilah and her tribe the Philistines were snared in God's awesome trap. They assisted in their own fate, and the judgment and the redemption of Samson. "For my thoughts are not your thoughts, neither are your ways my ways." (Isaiah 55:7, 8) I would like to draw reference at this time to Samson's plight and what Judas Iscariot did to betray the Lord Jesus Christ, to bring him to the great moment to die at Calvary, to shed his precious blood that would save believers upon the earth forever!

Deception and Victory

Delilah, her beauty and seductive ways has been talked about throughout time. The beautiful seductress that snared the great Samson. God had ordained Samson from birth to be victorious over his enemies. Samson's birth was God's answer to Israel's pain, suffering and prayers that they were going to be relieved out of the hands of their persecutors. Samson achieved many victories as he killed the Philistines. They knew him well and they plotted and planned for his capture and punishment. God laid Samson's path of victory against the Philistines, the locks of his hair held the blessing and mystery to his strength. This was the information that the Philistines sought in order to destroy Samson.

Samson was revered as a great warrior and he welcomed this position. However, his disobedient behavior led him to decadence and immoral acts in the sight of God, his family and his people. He held a weakness for Philistine women, enemies of his people, yet he took them as his wife. It was Delilah's womanly ways that made him submissive and under Delilah's control that coaxed Samson into revealing the secret of his strength. The Philistines used this information to capture and torture Samson and gouge out his eyes. They made a mockery of him and celebrated his captivity.

It is God who used Delilah to free Samson and Israel from persecution and hardship. The sight of her beauty and her alluring behavior seduced Samson. Although the Philistines took his sight, he saw his mission more clearly. His hair had grown back, and he prayed to God for redemption. He was able to deploy his task with his renewed strength and achieve victory by destroying the Philistines. Samson sought Delilah to satisfy his flesh; God used her to satisfy His plan. By keeping His promise to Israel and achieving victory over the Philistines, God's will is done!

Chapter Ten

The Story of RUTH

The biblical story of the Moabitish woman 'RUTH' is one of the world's oldest and romantic stories. It cannot be properly told or written about without making references to both the story of her beloved mother-in-law Naomi and her opulent and respected husband Boaz. Ruth is one of the most popular known stories of gentile women in the Bible.

Ruth means beauty. She was a Moabite young widow of Mahlon, the senior brother of Chilion of Elimelech and Naomi. Ruth was profoundly devoted to her widowed and desperate mother-in-law Naomi, for whom she voluntarily left her own people, to later become the glorious and legitimate wife of the religious, rich, generous, and notable Boaz of Bethlehem, in the land of Judah. (Ruth 1:1-5)

Moabites were descendants of Moab; he was the son of Lot and his oldest daughter, and also the great nephew of the patriarch and prophet Abraham. Though the Moabites were Israelites neighbors, they were very much hated by the early Israelites as idolatrous, wicked, and unclean. (Genesis 19:30-36)

"...Elimelech, Naomi's husband died, and she were left, and her two sons. And took them wives of the women of Moab; the name of the one was Orpah, and the name of the other Ruth: and they dwelled there about ten years. And Mahlon and Chilion died also both of them: and the woman was left of her two sons and her husband." (Ruth 1:3-5).

Elimelech who was from the tribe of Ephrath, his wife Naomi and their two lovely sons Mahlon and Chilion left Bethlehem in Judah for Moab. Because of the severe famine that visited their land they were unable to stay. This is where Elimelech died.

Ruth met Mahlon, a young Jew, and fell in love and got married. After ten good years of marriage, Ruth's husband suddenly died leaving her without a child from his loin. Ruth suffered hardship upon the death of her husband Mahlon. Her sister-in-law Orpah who married her husband's younger brother Chilion also lost her husband to death, and she did not have a child from her husband's loins. This is considered the saddest and the most embarrassing occurrence in these young couple's lives. It was Ruth's widowed mother-in-law Naomi that Ruth sought consolation, protection, love and understanding from, as she faced a doubtful and desolate future. This would be the moment that the young widow Ruth would make a wise and final decision.

The old and tired Naomi firmly faced her fate of a widowed woman in the eastern family; and she longed to return to the land of her birth. Ruth and Orpah first started out their journey to Bethlehem with the depressed Naomi. On the way, Naomi pleaded with her daughters-in-law to return to their mother's house and fulfill their destiny, to marry again and bear children. Orpah finally did turn back to her family in Moab, but it was Ruth's decision to faithfully stay with Naomi.

"And they lifted up their voice, and wept again: and Orpah kissed her mother-in-law; but Ruth clave unto her. And she said, behold, thy sister-in-law is gone back unto her people, and unto her gods: return thou after thy sister-in-law. And Ruth said,

Intreat me not to leave thee, or to return from following after thee: for whither thou goest, I will go; and where thou lodgest, I will lodge: thy people shall be my people, and thy God my God: Where thou diest, will I die, and there will I be buried: the Lord do so to me, and more also, if ought but death part thee and me. (Ruth 1:14-17)

Ruth's emotional expression was out of Godly compassion and love. She faithfully made that unprecedented and unselfish choice to be by Naomi's side until death. The beautiful, young, humble, sober, and intelligent Ruth and her old, experienced, and wise mother-in-law turned their faces toward Palestine to go back to her old home and relatives, with anticipation to profit from the good harvest of her people during the year. They finally arrived in Bethlehem and were welcomed by her kindred people.

When they safely reached Bethlehem, Ruth, in order to support herself and her old and weary mother-in-law, cleverly found her way and followed the reapers and gathered up the fragments of grain that fell to the ground, that were left behind for the poor to collect for their meals. Without fear of this difficult task and the least feeling of self-pity, Ruth gleaned everyday in the scorching sun, returning home at the end of the day, always happy with the little harvest she had for her and Naomi. Fortunately, one day Ruth came upon a field belonging to a renowned, rich, and religious landowner, namely Boaz; he was a near kinsman of Naomi. That is where Ruth continued to glean grain for her and Naomi's survival. She went about this task humbly, quietly and made out very well.

"And Boaz answered and said unto her, It hath fully been shewed me, all that thou hast done unto thy mother-in-law since the death of thine husband: and how thy hast left thy father and thy mother, and the land of thy nativity, and art come unto a people which thou knewest not heretofore. The Lord recompense thy work, and a full reward be given thee of the Lord God of Israel, under whose wings thou art come to trust." (Ruth 2:11-12)

Ruth happily kept her promise and commitment to her old, tired, and wise mother-in-law Naomi. She supported her with genuine kindness, humility, respect, joy, and love. Hence the Lord God rewarded her through Boaz's appreciation, generosity, hospitality and protection. The godly and spirited Boaz, recognized Ruth's beauty, her quietness, loveliness, kindness, courtesy, devotion and hard working efforts, and he admired her.

The religious and generous Boaz advised the smart and hardworking Ruth, not to worry herself to go to other small fields to pick up grain that she should continue to come to glean in his large fields throughout the harvest. Anytime she came to the field to pick up grain, he invited her to come and eat bread and put her food in his sauce and drink from the water jars they had filled. The Hebrew affectionate Boaz kindly served Ruth some roasted grain to eat and sent the leftovers to her home, to Naomi. He again strongly warned his reapers in the field not to speak harshly to her, but rather allow her to pick up grain from areas where others had been forbidden to glean from or pick from his own storage. Boaz would at times pass parched grain to Ruth and also instructed his reapers or aiders to pull out some stalks from their bundles and leave them for her to make her gleanings more convenient and plenteous. (Ruth 2:8-9, 14-15).

The intelligent and honest Ruth always reported to her mother-in-law and very honored matron Naomi what happened between her and the rich, kind, and respected Boaz. Boaz's attentions to Ruth, were made known to Naomi through her humble and beloved daughter-in law Ruth's stories. For this reason, this encouraged Naomi to start a plan that would help to make her grateful and lovable Ruth happy. She would now know the power and the miracle of the great God of Israel and finally help to preserve or maintain the family name and estate for future generations. Ruth's sincere good-hearted nature, hard work, care, and love for the poor and desperate Naomi was abundantly compensated.

Naomi clearly knew very well that, if a man dies without an heir, the Levirate law requires the brother to marry the widow as in the case of both her husband and her two sons. She seriously and respectfully advised Ruth to wash, and anoint herself with quality and expensive perfume, then to put her best and attractive clothing on, and to go where Boaz was after he had finished eating and drinking. She intentionally directed Ruth to the threshing floor where the sympathetic Boaz would be selecting or separating his grain at night.

Naomi said to Ruth, "And it shall be, when he lieth down, that thou shalt mark the place where he shall lie, and thou shalt go in, and uncover his feet, and lay there down; and he will tell thee what thou shalt do. Ruth, knowing that her mother-in-law would command her to do nothing that was not considered proper, replied, "All that thou sayest unto me I will do." (Ruth 3:4-5)

What a wise and a cunning advice from a beloved, experienced and bold mother-in-law to give to her humble, studious, and smart daughter-in-law. The honorable Boaz sincerely agreed to the servile, clever and bold approach of Ruth. He considered her behavior to seek his legal protection, care, and love as an obligation and profound honor to him. It was a peculiar and an ancient custom that Ruth, assisted by Naomi used to make this noble demand. Boaz courteously and patiently understood and received the vulnerable Ruth and they discussed the prospect of marriage. However, Boaz must first consult the nearer kinsman in the family and also seek the witnessing and approval of the elders and the entire people.

Then said Boaz, "What day thou buyest the field of the hand of Naomi, thou must buy it also of Ruth the Moabitess, the wife of the dead, to raise up the dead upon his inheritance. And the kinsman said, I cannot redeem it for myself, lest I mar mine own inheritance: redeem thou my right to thyself; for I cannot redeem it_____ Therefore the kinsman said unto Boaz, buy it for thee. So he drew off his shoes." (Ruth 4:5-6)

According to the custom in those days, to make a sale legal, one person would take off a sandal or shoe and give it to the other. Therefore, after the kinsman had agreed to let Boaz buy the property, he took off one of his shoes and handed it to Boaz. Without any hesitation the wise Boaz told the town leaders and everyone about the kinsman's refusal to purchase from Naomi the property of her deceased husband Elimelech and his two sons, and his intention to marry the Moabite woman, the widow Ruth.

"And Boaz said unto all the people, Ye are witnesses this day, that I have bought all that was Elimelech's and all that was Chilion's and Mahlon's, of the hand of Naomi. Moreover, Ruth the Moabitess, the wife of Mahlon, have I purchased to be my wife, to raise up the name of the dead upon his inheritance, that the name of the dead be not cut off from among his brethren, and from the gate of his place: ye are witnesses this day." (Ruth 4:9-10)

The highly respected, rich, religious, and land proprietor Boaz went forth publicly to declare that he had bought from Naomi, the property that belonged to Elimelech and his two sons. Boaz again delightfully made it known that he had also agreed to legally marry Mahlon's widow Ruth, the Moabitess. So the generous Boaz brought the lovely and grateful Ruth into the family of God's chosen people. Through Ruth's loveliness, faithfulness, industry, humbleness, commitment, patience and above all her perseverance brought her out of sorrow and poverty to joy and prosperity. Both the elders and the people in the city of Bethlehem were exceedingly pleased with the result, for they very much respected the godly, kind and noble Boaz and had also heard only good things about the lovely and beautiful Moabitish damsel Ruth. For this reason, they sincerely prayed and wished both the bride and groom many blessings.

Soon after Boaz and Ruth's glorious marriage, Obed was born. Ruth was assured before the birth of her son Obed that, her child's name would be "famous in Israel." Ruth 4:14). Noami's neighbors named the child "Obed." Simply because the child was the son of her beloved daughter-in-law and that child would make her happy and also take care of her in her old age. Naomi was told that her daughter-in-law Ruth loved her more than seven sons of her own would love her. The rewarded and comforted Naomi greatly loved the child Obed who was also called "Naomi's boy," and she became a nurse to her beloved grandson. (Ruth 4:15-16)

Obed became famous and the grandfather of the great King David from whose house and lineage the Lord Jesus Christ was born. It is an honor and interesting to note that, besides the beautiful, cunning and courageous Tamar of Judah, Ruth was the second gentile woman of the Holy Bible who upon the old Levirate law, struggled to reinstate her womanhood, maintained the family name and property throughout the generations. Ruth's humility, sympathy, and love transcended the frontier of hatred and race, which is in our modern times wealthy of emulation. Ruth's name is an everlasting fragrance among the four Gentile women named in the genealogy of our Lord Jesus, the redeemer. Ruth from Moab, a gentile, showed her devout devotion to Naomi. She is accepted into Boaz's family and a child of their God.

God-Loving

The Moabitish Ruth loved Naomi, who introduced her to the God she served, taught her the custom of her people, and helped her through her mourning period over the demise of her husband. Ruth's spirit of commitment and loving actions toward Naomi show us her quality character and her true inner beauty. It was initiated through the belief and understanding of the God that Naomi served which surpassed the spiritual understanding that Ruth had prior to meeting Ruth's son Mahlon. Her faithful devotion inspired her mother-in law Naomi to develop a relationship and love for Ruth as if she were her own child, instead of a daughter-in law. The respect and belief in the God Naomi and her people served, the respect Ruth showed for their culture, and the honor she paid their God that she chose to be her God, brought her favor and acceptance amongst Naomi's kinfolk.

A Hebrew by the name of Boaz noticed Ruth and he studied her from afar as she went about her daily activities, she won his heart. Boaz was a religious man and very rich. Ruth as the God-chosen wife of the God serving Boaz, mother of Obed, grandmother of King David; her nurturing qualities are recognized as a wife, a mother and a grandmother qualifies her to be in the ancestry line of God's only Begotten Son. Ruth was a woman that demonstrated goodness in the actions of her daily life. What some may consider as self-sacrificial, was a state of being for Ruth. It is not a coincidence that these unseen forces worked together for God's will to be done through the God ordained lives of people like Naomi, Ruth, Boaz, Obed, King David and others; constructing the lineage of Jesus Christ, Our Lord and Savior today. It is with a revelation that we are able to review Ruth's rites of passage as a God-chosen human vessel played out with God's will, as presented in our most 'Holy Bible.'

Chapter Eleven

The Story of BATHSHEBA

The name Bathsheba denotes "daughter of the oath." She was a pretty and respectful daughter of Eliam also named Ammiel, which in Hebrew means, "God is gracious." Bathsheba was first married to one of her tribesmen called Uriah the Hittite. Uriah was a descendant of Heth, the son of Canaan of Ham, the great ancestor of Black and Colored people. (Genesis 10:1-20)

We know for sure that Bethsheba came from a God-fearing family. Her father Eliam was very religious and was also one of the doorkeepers of the Temple in Jerusalem. Bathsheba was also named Bathshhua and her beauty was beyond description. (Chronicles 3:5; 26:5) Her kind and very religious brother Machir who lived in the city of Lo-Debar first took care of

David's best friend Jonathan's only and disabled son named Mephibosheth that he left behind. (11 Samuel 9:3-5)

"And it came to pass in an evening tide, that David arose from off his bed, and walked upon the roof of the king's house and from the roof he saw a woman washing herself; and the woman was very beautiful to look upon. And David sent and inquired after the woman. And one said, Is not this Bathsheba, the daughter of Eliam, the wife of Uriah the Hittite?" (11 Samuel 11:2-3).

The scripture explains that, David the king of Israel, got up from bed one evening and started walking around on the flat roof of his palace. He saw a very beautiful young woman who was down below in her courtyard bathing as her religion demanded. David could not resist the temptation and immediately loved her. He sent his servants or messengers to inquire after Bathsheba, and as a result brought her to his palace and slept with her. Later, when Bathsheba found that she was going to have a child, she became afraid, disturbed and without any hesitation sent someone to King David with the following message: "I am with child." (11 Samuel 11:5).

According to both the law and custom of the land in those days, the beautiful Bathsheba had no right, even if it was against her wish, to refuse the will or offer of a great King like David. In those ancient times women were totally subject to a King's demand. It was a law that, if a King wanted a woman, he could have her without being questioned. For this reason, we would say that, as a married woman, Bathsheba had no choice to refuse the sexual aggression upon her by King David. The harsh message, which Bathsheba sent to David after she found out that she had a child, the profound grief she had and the mourning for her deceased husband Uriah, reflects that she was initially not happy with the sexual encounters in which King David had forced upon her.

"And David sent to Joab, saying, send me Uriah the Hittite. And Joab sent Uriah to David._____And David said to Uriah, Go down to thy house, and wash thy feet. And Uriah departed out of the King's house, and there followed him a mess of meat from the King. But Uriah slept at the door of the King's house with all the servants of his lord, and went not down to his house." (11 Samuel 11:6-9).

For King David to avoid judgment and disgrace, he first and intentionally called his General Uriah back home to Jerusalem and deceptively told him to go to his house without any explanation, to clean up and take a rest with his wife. However, Uriah being an experienced warrior, respectful, faithful and consecrated, refused the advice of the King and slept in the King's barracks with his guards and servants. David who was still zealous to involve Uriah in his wife Bathsheba's pregnancy, tried a second time to win or influence Uriah to go to see his wife Bathsheba. Again Uriah refused and humbly told the King that, "The ark, and Israel, and Juda, abide in tents; and my lord Joab, and the servants of my lord, are encamped in the open fields; shall I then go into mine house, to eat and drink, and lie with my wife? As thou livest, and as thy soul liveth, I will not do this thing." (11 Samuel 11:11).

Uriah was an honest, religious, and dedicated soldier. He had great respect for the law and the customs, which prohibited intercourse to soldiers who had been consecrated for battle. (1 Samuel 21:4-5; Proverbs 31:3). King David designed a more diabolic plan to get out of his dilemma, by making Uriah drunk, he was sure Uriah would lieth with his wife Bathsheba, but, the faithful and gallant warrior Uriah still did not give up to go down to his beloved wife Bathsheba. Finally, when David saw that all attempts had completely failed, he intensively sought to murder his innocent and great General Uriah the Hittite.

And it came to pass in the morning, that David wrote a letter to Joab, and sent it by the hand of Uriah. And he wrote in the letter, saying, Set ye Uriah in the forefront of the hottest battle, and retire ye from him, that he may be smitten, and die." (II Samuel 11:14-15).

In order to cover his crime of adultery with Bathsheba and get her for his wife, he ordered his commander-in-chief Joab, to place his general Uriah and his insufficient forces in the hottest part of the battle with Ammon, and then deserted him, leaving him to be conquered and slained by the enemies. (11 Samuel 11:16-17,23,24).

We accept that King David planned the crime, however, his chief commander Joab also connived and assisted him to see to it that, the mighty and faultless General Uriah would be killed in the battle. Though David's plot with Joab succeeded, however, it was Bathsheba who immensely suffered the lost of her husband in this incident, because King David had been overcome with lust and his heart was conquered by her beauty.

The Lord became very angry at what David had done with Bathsheba and sent Prophet Nathan to confront him in a very revealing parable. David who from the beginning did not know that he was the real offender, instantly after hearing Nathan's parable he became angry and swore that the culprit deserved to die. Nathan then, boldly told King David, "Thou art the man." (II Samuel 12:1-7) Prophet Nathan's condemnation of David as a result of his crime of adultery with Bathsheba and the deliberate murder of his great general Uriah, made King David cry out:

"Have mercy upon me O God, according to thy loving kindness: according unto the multitude of thy tender mercies blot out my transgressions. Wash me thoroughly from my sin. For I acknowledge my transgressions: and my sin is ever before me." (Psalm 51:1-3).

David's sins reflected a change in his victories and achievements and started trouble for his nation, his family and even in his personal life. The violation of David produced chastisement and confusion at every level. When their son, born of adultery died, as a punishment from the Lord God, David who was relieved and full of hope lamented by saying:

"But now he is dead, wherefore should I fast? Can I bring him back again? I shall go to him, but he shall not return to me." (II Samuel 12:23)

David repented and trusted the Lord after the death of his first son with Bathsheba of Uriah. He whole-heartedly agreed with his predecessor Job that, "Naked came I out of my mother's womb, and naked shall I return thither; the Lord gave, and the Lord hath taken away; blessed be the name of the Lord." (Job 1:21)

After the untimely death of Uriah, the beautiful and bereaved Bathsheba was brought into the palace of King David to be his most respected and beloved wife. King David comforted Bathsheba and again slept with her. Later on, she gave birth to another handsome baby boy and named him Solomon meaning, "the peaceful," a symbol that he was likely born after David rested from his numerous wars and lived in peace. Bathsheba was abundantly blessed and had a comfortable life because she was the favorite wife of David. Besides Solomon, David had another three sons with Bathsheba. They were Shimea, Shobab and Nathan. However, the Lord God loved Bathsheba's lovely son Solomon more than any of David's sons born with other wives. (1 Chronicles 3:1-9).

It is interesting and an honor to note that, in the genealogy of the Lord Jesus Christ, Bathsheba is gloriously mentioned as the former wife of Uriah the Hittite and mother of Solomon by David. (Matthew 1:6).

Though King David had many great sons and daughters. However, Solomon was the apple of his eye like his mother Bathsheba. Through prayer, intelligence, respect, meekness, intervention, and vision, Bathsheba succeeded in getting her beloved son Solomon to succeed his father as the King of Israel. Solomon who eventually became the famous and the wisest King ever lived on earth, in return, honored his beautiful, diligent, religious, diplomatic, and beloved mother as the respected queen mother of the kingdom of Israel. It is only a woman of courage, wisdom, and influence and with a dream who could have won such a great triumph for her son and herself.

Even today, Bathsheba's name exists as the godly mother of Israel's wisest King, the great ancestor of Jesus Christ, and the most beautiful and respected queen mother in biblical times.

Obedience and Honor

Bathsheba went as an obedient servant to King David's bed. Although her heart was yearning for her husband, she obeyed the culture and rules of the people. No one was to deny the request of a King. Her obedience to lay with King David at his bequest cost the life of her husband. But the story yields to the understanding of the power of lust and the betrayal of yourself and the lengths human frailty will allow us to go to satisfy those fleshly desires. Although king David knew better he did not do better. King David's lust opened the door for him to act upon performing other sins, such as, lying, deception, and ultimately murder.

King David's lustful and lying actions to have another man's wife, namely Bathsheba and the murder of his loyal servant, the husband of that wife, summoned God to correct him. Although

King David honored Bathsheba as his wife, he suffered immense guilt because of his behavior. But the dye had been cast and the iniquity that had been done was soon to return to King David. The child that Bathsheba carried for David died. King David's other son was disobedient and reaped bitter fruit towards his father. The second child between King David and Bathsheba was Solomon assured to be King. Bathsheba advocated for her son to rein as king. The promise of God with Abraham continues to be honored, as we witness God's will be done!

The Epilogue

The Bible references that woman was created from a man's rib. The scripture goes on to reflect that it was through Eve the woman that tempted man to disobeyed God, they both fell from grace and was cursed. Therefore, it is impossible for anyone to separate woman from man in God's plan of salvation. Man relies or yields to woman who is of his own bone and flesh to achieve his Godly purpose, blessings, and salvation. Woman is to obey man as God has directed, to express her womanly nurturing abilities upon her husband and children while guiding them toward fortifying their spiritual growth.

If the man is weak and disturbed, the woman is affected. Likewise, if the man is strong and happy, the woman is automatically affected. Our experience of Black and Colored Women in the Bible both in the past and at present has revealed and shown that women are able to be spiritually nurturing. A woman's duty is to assist her family in ascertaining their God-given qualities.

In the lives of these black and colored women presented here in this text, is the presence of God almighty at work. From Eve, to even Delilah, these women's godly path and their way of life reveal their depth, breadth, and significance (as gentiles) that God can only fathom. It has been shown that these women were wives, mothers, (and or) lovers, whores, harlots, and seducers of men. Our God used these women to fulfill His greatest purpose. They played significant roles in the lives of men that God had ordained as patriarchs, prophets, leaders, and kings. Excluding Delilah, whom is a Philistine, they are all in the ancestry bloodline of royalty, the Son of God, Jesus Christ our Lord and Savior.

For this reason, it is incumbent upon men to seriously invite and encourage women to assist them in all their endeavors. In the same spirit, women should also, effectively and lovingly support their male counterpart morally, spiritually, physically, and economically.

It is not by mistake for our Holy God in the beginning to create both man and woman's relationship to be partners of each other. God deemed that they have relationship with each other and live in authority over the planet; to care, support and love as they adhere to the sacred commandments of God. If a man is the reservoir of life, woman is the vehicle of life.

Hence, a man and a woman authored this famous book. They worked together to the fulfillment of what God has ordained man to do. The objective is to work together in a partnership creating a greater good for man's existence upon earth. Any individual who makes a choice to pick up this precious book to read, we pray that they are purged by the spirit of God and blessed with the understanding that Black and Colored Women were significant vessels. These women were used as vessels, to create a passage for Christ Jesus to be born, to cover man's sins with his blood; man's sins through the blood of Christ are forgiven. It is finished.

Charles Aka & Theresa Liptrot

About the Authors

Dr. Aka was born in West Africa, Ghana, and although he misses his native homeland, he feels that he was destined to pursue his dreams in America. He attended Teachers Training College for four years and later earned a doctorate degree in religion. He has been ministering for over thirty years and has presided as a Pastor over the Evangelical Church of Christ, which is a spiritual movement in West Africa; he was the national President in Africa for the Restored Church of Jesus Christ, and the Church of God of Prophecy. His many affiliations and active leadership has earned him the experience to author such books as; Who Are The True Children and the Church of God; Choosing God or Satan's Standards on Earth; Back to the Early Church; The Motherland of Humanity: A Handbook of Africa and Bill Clinton: Man of the Public. Dr. Aka is presently ministering at The Fellowship Chapel in Bronx, New York. He and his late wife Salomey Korkor Aka's union were blessed with nine children. He lives in Bronx, New York City.

Theresa Artemus-Liptrot is the seventh child of Rose Lee (Norris) Artemus. She is the honored wife of Kenneth Ross Liptrot for twenty-three years; he is her soul mate and has always been her strongest supporter in many of her endeavors. Theresa and Kenneth were blessed to be surrogate parents and earned many years of life's experience by nurturing others. Her and Kenneth's life as native New Yorkers, continues to be blessed as they pursue their life's journey on this earth, together. In the awesome passage of birthing this creative manuscript as a co-author of Black and Colored Women of the Bible, the experience has been spirit filled. It has allowed Theresa to have a closer relationship with God; an accomplishment that she deems has surpassed her formal educational achievement of earning a Master's of Art degree from Brooklyn College. She has worked as an administrator, teacher, and counselor for substance abusers. She and her family presently reside in Brooklyn, New York.

www.ingramcontent.com/pod-product-compliance
Lightning Source LLC
Chambersburg PA
CBHW051421280526
45785CB00003B/1107